Three Littl

A True Story of Hope . . .

Three Little Birds

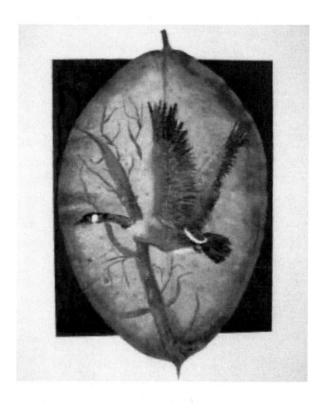

A True Story of Hope...

by
Rick Steber

Cover design by Gary Asher
Page layout by Jody Conners

ISBN 978-0-945134-46-6

Books by Rick Steber

Rendezvous
Traces
Union Centennial
Where Rolls the Oregon
Heartwood
Oregon Trail – Last of the Pioneers
Roundup
New York to Nome
Wild Horse Rider
Buckaroo Heart
No End in Sight
Buy the Chief a Cadillac
Legacy
Forty Candles
Secrets of the Bull
Caught in the Crosshairs
A Promise Given
Red White Black
All-Around and the 13th Juror
A Better Man
Three Little Birds

Tales of the Wild West Series
Oregon Trail
Pacific Coast
Indians
Cowboys
Women of the West
Children's Stories
Loggers
Mountain Men
Miners
Grandpa's Stories
Pioneers
Campfire Stories
Tall Tales
Gunfighters
Grandma's Stories
Western Heroes

www.ricksteber.com

After a devastating forest fire a logger was walking through a blackened meadow and came across the charred remains of a Canada goose still on her nest. The sight was sickening—the outside feathers had turned to ash and the scorched meat gave off a repulsive stench—and yet the logger used a stick to gently roll the bird off the nest. A pair of yellow goslings scurried from under their mother. In the heat of the advancing fire the mother could have abandoned her nest and flown away to safety. She chose to gather her babies under her wings to protect them from the flames. She was willing to die so her offspring might live.

He will cover you with His feathers,
and under His wings you will find refuge.
(Psalm 91: 4)

Dedication

To the memory of Jonathan Ashley Thomas Brown; the medical staff at the hospitals where organs are recovered, and transplants take place; and to all those who make the conscious decision to become organ donors.

George and Silly Little Goose (Tootie)

"Three Little Birds"
Bob Marley

*Don't worry about a thing
'Cause every little thing gonna be alright
Singin' don't worry about a thing
'Cause every little thing gonna be alright*

*Rise up this mornin'
Smiled with the risin' sun
Three little birds
Pitch by my doorstep
Singin' sweet songs
Of melodies pure and true
Sayin' this is my message to you*

*Singin' don't worry 'bout a thing
'Cause every little thing gonna be alright
Singin' don't worry 'bout a thing
'Cause every little thing gonna be alright*

Sprague River

Far away in the remote mountains of south central Oregon there are hidden lava tubes and inconspicuous fault lines that allow underground water to bubble to the surface. Out in the overwhelming crush of forest silence, these springs gurgle forth and feed pools of lively green watercress. Long legged water skippers glide across the dappled mirrored plane. Water leaks, tumbles, plunges from these hidden pools, flashing past cinnamon barked ponderosa pine and thickets of tightly packed lodgepole pine. Trickles and rivulets join forces, come crashing and ripping their way down draws and ravines, always in a hurry, always in a rush. But occasionally the cold waters linger, flowing in gentle and circuitous paths across alpine meadows carpeted with a profusion of vibrant and sweet smelling wildflowers. Mule deer graze here. Songbirds flit about, calling out lyrical cords and sometimes caustically repetitive tunes. A cougar slinks silently into view and quickly fades into the landscape like the passing of a fanciful gust of wind. A black bear waddles across a narrow opening, slips into a finger of timber and is gone. Only on rare occasions does man appear as an intruder in this deeply forested wilderness.

North Fork of Sprague River is born in the high reaches of Gearhart Mountain, west of Winter Rim and east of the confines of Summer Lake Basin. Off to the north is the bald face of Yamsay Mountain dividing Sprague River from the Williamson River drainage. South Fork of Sprague River is formed by low mountains that block and separate the flows of Lost River and the many small tributaries feeding Goose Lake. After the two branches of Sprague River join forces they take their own sweet time weaving back and forth across a broad basin of alluvial bottomlands formed millions of years ago by volcanic eruptions and catastrophic faults that moved the land up and down and twisted huge chunks at odd angles. By this point in the river's journey the conifer forests have transitioned to sagebrush and juniper steppes. The broad meadow corridor through which the hundred-mile-long river passes is vegetated with lush grasses and wetlands that were used for thousands of years as an ideal stopover and nesting area for Canada geese and other migrating waterfowl.

In more recent geological times the Sprague River watershed was profoundly affected by the eruption of Mount Mazama, more than 7,000 years ago. This terrifying explosion changed the lives of the Native People—Klamath, Modoc, and Yahooskin Tribes. Historically they had used the high country for hunting and gathering during the warm weather months and existed in winter camps pitched along Sprague River, but after the devastating eruption they were forced to move to where the deposits of ash and fallout were not as deep. They returned to their old haunts when vegetation began to grow, game had returned to the mountains and fish once more came upriver to spawn.

The first white explorer to the basin country was Peter Skeen Ogden in 1826. He led a band of Hudson's Bay trappers in search of beaver pelts. Twenty years later wagon pioneers were crossing the Oregon Trail and flooding into the Willamette Valley. As the Valley became populated, enterprising souls pushed south and eastward into the Sprague and Klamath basins. A military outpost was established at Fort Klamath and in 1864 the Native People were forced onto a one million-acre reservation. The passing of the Dawes Act of 1887 allowed for individual allotments to be made to tribal members, resulting in much of the richest land along the Sprague River being sold and passing from tribal lands into private ownership. In 1954, the Klamath Tribes voted for "termination," and each enrolled member received a cash settlement of $43,000. The former reservation lands passed to the federal government and were incorporated into the Fremont and Winema National Forests.

The common threads stitching together the following true story: a goose egg rescued from a nest along Sprague River, a man with a damaged heart who hatches the special egg, the steadfast love of a caring woman for her husband, and a young man who, in death, gives the ultimate gift, the gift of life.

Foreword

It was yet another one of those fabulous late fall days the San Francisco Peninsula is so famous for—sunshine and 88 degrees—but once the sun set into the distant curve of the Pacific Ocean, that open canopy of sky allowed the temperature to plummet to an overnight low of 54 degrees.

At 2:22 a.m. on October 17, 2008, the 911 dispatch center received a call of an accident involving two vehicles on a rural mountain road near Los Gatos. California Highway Patrol responded. The initial investigation indicated a 1987 Mazda RX-7 had crossed the center line and glanced off a second vehicle, sending two men with non-life-threatening injuries to a hospital in San Francisco. After striking the vehicle, the Mazda had continued on and crashed head-on into a tree. The driver, a young man, was unconscious and unresponsive. He was transported by helicopter to the Level One Trauma Unit at Santa Clara Valley Medical Center in San Jose. It was here that a team of doctors determined the victim had suffered the most severe of all injuries, an irreversible, catastrophic brain injury. All brain functions had ceased. The victim had no identification, but every member in the trauma unit knew full well that as the sun rose on yet another day of perfect weather, there was a family out there in the awakening world who would soon be devastated to learn of this tragedy involving their precious son.

For the immediate future, the doctors and staff would do everything possible for the unidentified patient—supporting blood pressure and heart rate with medications and using a breathing ventilator and other life support measures when they became necessary. As soon as the victim could be identified, and the family notified, then a collective decision would have to be made concerning the possibility of recovering the healthy organs that would thereby extend the lives of many others who were in desperate need.

One Bird

Donna Hooker

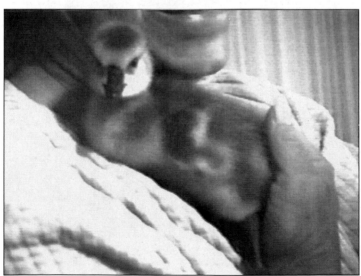

Donna Hooker and Silly Little Goose

Silly Little Goose,
age one month

House Goose

'They're social, loving, very interesting. She knows
words. They're so sweet ..., and they love so much.
I don't think she knows she's a goose."
— Donna Hooker

*"Herald and
News" story*

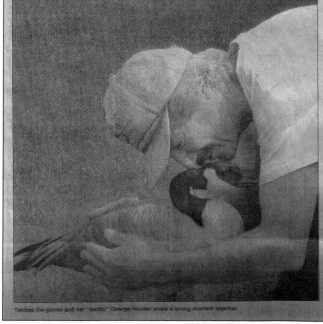

Tootsie the goose and her "daddy" George Hooker share a loving moment together

3

Chapter One

It was an unusually warm spring day with a high blue sky and a few fluffy clouds traipsing off to the east. As Donna Hooker drove the ribbon of highway hugging the twists and turns of the lazy Sprague River, she had a lot on her mind. Typically she enjoyed the drive home from work, but on this particular afternoon she was preoccupied.

Donna's husband, George, had been learning to live with type 2 diabetes, controlling it to some degree with a strict diet, regular exercise, blood sugar monitoring, medication and insulin therapy. Lately he had been experiencing alarming sensations in his chest; his heart fluttered, sometimes slowing way down until he hardly had enough energy to move, and at other times speeding up and beating so fast he feared it might thump right out of his chest.

George had always been active. He worked hard and spent his free time rebuilding old cars, hiking, hunting and fishing. He was a handy man to have around the house and could fix most anything, but his deteriorating health had gradually limited his activities until he had been forced to, reluctantly, quit working and go on disability. From living a comfortable existence when they were both working, George and Donna learned to tighten their financial belt and live on George's disability check and what Donna could earn on the side.

Donna was 51. She had red hair, a quiet, pleasant face and expressive blue eyes. Her smile told when she was happy— which was most of the time. She had learned to hide her emotions when she was anxious or afraid. She hated to have to spend so much time away from George, especially since the doctors in Klamath Falls had finally diagnosed his heart irregularities as something extremely grave—cardiomyopathy, a degenerative heart disease. The prognosis was that, in a few years, maybe sooner, George's heart would fail him. If he was on the organ donor list at that time, and lucky enough that a matching heart was located, he would get a new lease on life. If not, he would die. It was as simple as that. George was running on borrowed time, and every minute Donna was not with him, she felt, was a minute stolen from their lives.

It was Donna who was forced to pick up the slack. She did more, and more, and more. She drove George to doctor appointments, set out his daily medications, and made the 90-mile emergency runs to the E.R. when George experienced a health crisis. She fed the chickens and gathered eggs, cooked, did household chores and still worked a full-time job. At the end of each long day, she fell into bed completely exhausted. One thing she always looked forward to was the drive to and from work. Yet with every mile she traveled, she felt the unpleasant tugs of regret and guilt at having to be separated from George.

What if he had another *episode* while she was away? She would never forgive herself.

Donna felt an involuntary cry coming on and reached for the box of tissue she kept at the ready for these almost daily occurrences. At this point on her drive, the Sprague River makes a big, looping bend, coming very near to the highway. The pussy willows that lined the cutback above the water were budding as little puffs of white, but no leaves were sprouting, not yet. However, grasses were growing and that gave the area between road and river an almost park-like appearance. Donna sniffled and dabbed with a tissue at the corners of her leaky eyes.

As she blinked, her peripheral vision caught movement; a Canada goose wildly flapping its wings, as if trying to launch itself into flight. Behind the goose, very near, was a furry thing, just a blur of motion. Donna's first thought was, "Darn dog." She thought a dog was chasing the goose. But there were no houses nearby where a pet dog would reside. It had to be a coyote; very sleek, very fast, deadly in its intentions to kill the goose. Donna brought the car to an abrupt stop, threw open the door and stood outside the car yelling at the coyote. The coyote paid no mind and continued its chase. Donna stepped around the front of the car and took a few tentative steps onto the strip of grass. She waved her arms madly and shrieked at the coyote to stop.

The coyote, now even with the goose, turned its head and took a toothy bite, but got nothing more than a mouthful of feathers. The goose dodged and reversed its path. The coyote was much faster. It leaped on the back of the goose and seized the long, graceful neck in its vicious mouth. The goose went down, making a pitiful squawk and a splutter that sounded very much like air whooshing from a balloon. The coyote whipped the goose's neck back and forth, one way and then the other, crushing the thin stem of muscle and bone.

Donna charged straight ahead. Somewhere in that mad dash she had the presence of mind to arm herself with a stone, picking it up off the ground and hurling it at the coyote while screaming, "Get out of here! Get out of here!"

The stone glanced off the coyote's rump. It gave a sharp yip, dropped the goose and ran away. Donna rushed to the goose. She bent over the bird and petted the smooth, shiny feathers. The goose thrashed its spindly legs a time or two and gave a shudder that raced through its body like a ship running aground on rocks. Then the goose lay still and Donna watched life flicker from the black iris of one open eye. For just an instant a tiny glitter of light prevailed and then it went away, replaced with a filmy dullness that made Donna as sad as she had ever felt in her life.

At that moment, Donna felt she was incapable of helping anything or anyone —not the goose, and not George either. God was going to take George. She knew that. There was nothing she could do to save him, just as there had been nothing she could have done to save the goose.

Donna noticed a low-slung nest built down among the roots of the nearby willows. It was oval shaped, not especially deep and lined with leaves, small sticks and branches. To soften and cushion the nest, gray feathers and white down had been added—a thin blanket of insulation—tiny feathers from the body of the mother goose. Donna was heartbroken for the goose and angry as hell at the coyote. It had killed a mother that was simply sitting on a nest and trying to protect her eggs, her babies.

The nest was empty. The violent attack must have caused the eggs to have been kicked from the nest and topple into the cold river. But Donna's desperate sadness turned to joyfulness when she saw, nestled down among the twisted willow roots, an oblong sphere; eggshell white, mottled with brown and speckles of gray. One egg remained. She reached for it, fingers blindly closing around the egg. She picked it up and held it to her like a mother holding her newborn.

The egg was heavy and longer than the palm of Donna's hand. It was absolutely absurd, but at that moment it seemed to Donna as if the egg that she held so tightly to her body was pulsing with unseen life. Ridiculous. How could life be felt or even sensed inside the hard, yet ever so fragile eggshell? She guessed it was simply a case of her overactive imagination.

"What do I do with this egg?"

Should she put it back in the nest, or leave it beside the dead mother? Donna could not bring herself to do either. She just could not, would not. As soon as she left, the coyote would return, along with a host of scavengers—raccoons, weasels, eagles, hawks, ravens and magpies—and they would feast on the goose and damned if Donna was going to allow the egg to be part of that prolonged tragedy. She would take the egg home. George would know what to do.

George Hooker

George and Silly Little Goose, age one day

Silly Little Goose, age two weeks

George and Silly Little Goose, age two days

Silly Little Goose, age three weeks

Two Birds

Silly Little Goose, painting on a leaf by Donna Hooker

Chapter Two

George Hooker wore his hair long and bushy. He was 51 years old, and white was now beginning to creep across his scalp, making his head look like a mountain with a dusting of fresh snow. His eyebrows and mustache were like thick slashes of black. He was thin, gaunt really, and yet he was still able to wear his feelings on display like a proud general wears a chest-full of polished medals. If George was asked to describe his personality, he would undoubtedly grin, shrug and drawl, "At heart, I'm just a country boy."

It was that country boy heart that was failing George, and while his body adjusted to the medication prescribed by doctors to treat his cardiomyopathy, he had been advised to do nothing to tax his heart. He was resting in bed the day his wife, Donna, came home with an incredible story about witnessing a coyote attacking and killing a goose. She opened her hands and there was a freckled goose egg. She confessed, "I couldn't just leave it."

George took the egg. He had seen goose eggs before. This egg had some heft to it and George figured that, more than likely, there was a well developed baby bird inside the egg. He made a snap decision and announced, "Hell, I'm not doing anything else, maybe I'll become Goose Daddy and hatch this egg."

George slipped the egg under the covers, allowing it to rest on the center of his breastbone just above his damaged heart. He thought his body temperature could not be much different than that of a mother goose. If he kept the egg warm, rotated it like a goose on the nest will do, and sprinkled a little water on the shell from time to time to keep it malleable, the darn thing just might hatch. It was odd, but that simple positive act of caring for an egg gave George something he had needed lately in his life—a goal. For weeks and weeks, George had been living in the here and now; minute to minute, with no guarantees for another tomorrow.

George dozed on and off through the night and the egg remained where it was. In the morning, as Donna left for work, she leaned over George to kiss him goodbye and his hands instinctively moved to protect the egg.

George remained in bed and that afternoon he heard an unusual sound. At first he assumed a friend had come to visit and was walking down the long hallway. He called, but there was no answer. The sound abruptly stopped. George fell asleep, only to be awakened by the same sound again. It was a soft tap-tap-tap. Again he called, and again received no answer. He thought there must be a simple explanation. A gray squirrel was on the roof playing, or maybe a raven was trying to break a nut, or one of the deer that had become almost tame was rubbing its antlers on a nearby tree. Tap-tap-tap. What could that be? And then he felt the egg reposition itself on his chest, rolling to one side a tiny fraction of an inch. That movement startled George. He touched the egg and felt a tap-tap-tap on his fingertips. He inhaled sharply. It was almost a gasp as it dawned on him that the baby goose inside the egg was trying to peck its way to freedom. And now George was more excited about the present, and the immediate future, than he had been about anything in a long, long time.

He pulled back the covers, exposing the egg. He examined it carefully and could clearly see a small bump on the speckled shell where it appeared something from inside was attempting to push outward. Again came the tap-tap-tap and George could feel the vibrations with his fingertips. His thinking shifted and he remembered reports that after the Japanese attack on Pearl Harbor, for days after, the rescue crews could hear the tapping of men trapped in the hull of the overturned ships. He wondered if those vibrations could be felt on the iron skin of the ship. As the air supply dwindled, the tapping became more and more faint. World War II happened before George was born, but he had heard that story and the sadness of knowing men had been trapped inside the ships had stuck with him.

Tap-tap-tap. The tapping from the egg seemed to be getting stronger, more insistent. George inspected the bump on the shell and could clearly see a hole, a very small break on the hard eggshell. He stared at it for several long minutes but nothing happened, nothing changed. The egg was quiet. The baby goose inside was resting, gathering its strength.

George felt his heart beating faster and tried to relax. The doctors had advised him not to do anything that might overtax his heart. He was fearful, and then he felt his heart rate begin to slow and was relieved. With Donna away, this was not the time for an *episode*. The egg would take hours to hatch. He just had to be patient.

Rather than have eggshells in his bed, George took a hand towel from the nightstand and carefully placed it between the egg and his chest. He had already pulled down the covers because he did not want heat to sap the baby bird's strength. It would need every bit of muscle and power it could muster to chip its way out of the shell.

George wondered what that little bird inside the egg could possibly be thinking. Where did the instinct come from that told the baby the time had come to free itself? How did it know to use the egg tooth, a little spur on the end of the beak that would fall off after a day or two, to chip away at the inside of the egg? George thought if a person did not believe in God, or at least a higher being, that person should hold an egg that is hatching. Some power was lending a hand. George was sure of that. He could almost sense the determination, the resolve, the grit of the bird to enter the world of life. Call it willpower, fortitude, perseverance, but it was something. Was it courage, or perhaps bravery? George doubted it. Sure, it took a certain amount of both courage and bravery for the goose to peck its way into a world it could not begin to comprehend, but that was not it. The answer centered on one thing and one thing only—the power of instinctual behavior. It was instinct, and instinct alone that directed the baby bird to break apart the locked doors of the eggshell.

George drifted to sleep and dreamed he was in a park—there was a manicured lawn and a pond—and he was watching a full-grown Canada goose waddle to the water's edge and step in, buoyantly treading water with webbed feet. While on land the goose had seemed awkwardly out of place, but now it had reached a graceful equilibrium. Moving through the blue-green water the sleek gray bird was deliberate; each kick of a leg propelled the goose forward. Water swelled against the breast feathers and twin ripples made a V from the sides of the goose like windblown contrails slipping down the sky.

George woke up. He examined the egg once more and the tiny hole he had watched had grown in size. He could now distinguish movement inside the egg. He could not recognize beak or head or body—the hole in the egg was not big enough for that—all he saw was a blurred shifting. Tap-tap-tap. More of the brittle eggshell fell away and exposed to view a tiny fraction of black. George supposed it was a beak. From what he could observe, the beak—if it indeed was a beak—was shiny and had a look like hard plastic. For a long time there was no movement and the hole in the egg remained exactly the same.

Again George felt his heart accelerate. He told himself to calm down as he glanced at his watch and vowed not to look at the egg again for 30 minutes. He had no idea that this egg hatching business could be such a time consuming and stimulating experience. George told himself the egg would hatch in its own sweet time. Nothing was to be gained fussing over it. He had to be patient and just allow Mother Nature to run her course.

What George now anticipated was that the baby would hatch and he would feed the gosling and watch it grow to adulthood and then it would fly away and join a flock of migrating Canada geese. He viewed his part in the saga as merely lending a helping hand, and nothing more. The goose was not going to be a pet, not a companion or anything of the sort. It was a thing, just a thing. Then George allowed himself the indulgence of seeing the goose twice a year as it migrated north, and then south. It would drop from a long V of other geese and walk around squawking loudly. George and Donna would stand together and be thrilled the goose remembered them. After a few minutes the goose would fly away. As far as dreams go, it was a pleasant fantasy for George to imagine.

George looked at his watch and only 10 minutes had passed. The gosling was again working on the eggshell and George busied himself trying to contemplate all the goose might experience in its lifetime. He had heard that geese in the wild can live to be as old as 20 years. That was on the high side. He remembered that Canada geese mate for life. He thought that was sweet; just like he and Donna. They had found each other and the goose would find a mate too. And when his goose found a mate they would wander from the tundra of the Far North in the summer and to Mexico in the cold weather months. There would be storms to ride out and predators to avoid. There would be times of plenty and other times when food was in short supply. There would be hunters dressed in camouflage, enticing unwary birds with calls and lifelike decoys. It seemed to George that a goose's life was fraught with danger. He thought some about airplanes, and power lines, cars and trucks and trains. High winds could push a flock of migrating geese miles and miles away from their intended route. How did they know where to go, when to go?

More than 30 minutes had passed and a partial line had been cut in a semi-circle around one end of the egg. Several chunks of eggshell had broken away and now exposed to view was a feeble head—yellow/brown, wet and matted—a beak as black as coal, legs, long webbed feet. Although the little bird could now be seen crammed inside, that hole was clearly not large enough to allow for the bird to escape.

The baby rested, but even in rest its head twitched and jerked pathetically. It seemed beyond any possibility that the spindly, spastic bird could complete the job, chip away the remaining shell and break from its tight confinement.

The little bird gave a faint *cheep* and struggled mightily, throwing its head upward and back and kicking with its feet. With the sound of the lone chirp resonating, George felt an irresistible urge to pick away at the shell and free the laboring baby. But George knew better. This was nature's way. The bird had to expend the energy if it was to grow strong. And yet George tugged at the rough corners of the shell to see if any lose pieces might come apart easily. They did not. The eggshell was brittle and yet it had an amazing capacity to retain its oval shape. George had to remind himself—all in due time, all in due time.

The baby goose alternated between resting and thrashing. *Cheep-cheep-cheep*. George spoke and reassured the little bird that everything was going to be all right. The bird cheeped again and struggled even more mightily.

George had placed the hatching egg on a towel on the bed and now he lay propped on a cocked elbow, head cradled in one hand, watching the slow drama unfold. The baby was talking constantly, flaying its head about and attempting to gain a point of leverage. Stubby wings thrashed. Spindly legs kicked. At last George felt compelled to intervene. He took hold of the bottom half of the egg, held it up, and with gravity at work the baby found a point of purchase. The gosling spilled from the egg and onto the towel; muscles contracted in an undignified series of spasms; jerks, twitches, uncontrollable shudders and convulsions. It fought diligently and little by little, over time, the gosling gained enough muscle control so it could hold its head upright. Lying with its long neck extended, the face of the gosling—if George was reading it right—appeared to be one of total astonishment. George was not sure if the gosling was astonished at the world around it, or bewildered at the hatching process. Either way, he was sure the gosling was capable of processing thought and expressing its reaction.

By the time Donna arrived home from work the little bird was snuggled inside George's flannel shirt, and George was doing something he had not done for a very long time. He was sitting in his leather reclining chair in the living room, his feet propped up. George was supporting the bird with a hand. When Donna came in and saw George she immediately wanted to know, "What are you doing up?"

"Just felt like it."

The male voice that had encouraged the baby goose during the hatching process proved to be a trigger and the gosling stuck its head from the V of George's shirt and loudly proclaimed, *Cheep-cheep-cheep*.

"It hatched!" Donna held out her hands and George dutifully lifted the gosling from inside his shirt and carefully handed it to Donna. She marveled at the pretty gosling; the yellow fuzz on its belly and milk chocolate fuzz on its back. The wings were short and stumpy, the legs long and the feet ridiculously large. She held the gosling to her face and cooed. "You are so pretty. You pretty little goose."

The gosling lifted its head. *Cheep-cheep-cheep*.

"Have you named it?"

"I don't know if it's a boy or a girl, so I've been calling it Silly Little Goose because it's so silly. It won't let me out of its sight, and it keeps cheeping."

Donna had been holding Silly Little Goose in the palms of her two hands, but upon hearing George's voice, the gosling began struggling and continued to struggle until Donna handed the gosling back to George. Silly Little Goose snuggled against George's neck and was quiet and content.

George was smiling with the pride of a new father. He said, "The hatching was an ordeal; took forever. Guess we've got ourselves a new pet."

"What will we do with it?"

"Raise it," said George matter-of-factly, "and when it can fend for itself, we'll turn it loose."

"You seem pretty attached already. Are you sure you'll be able to let go when the time comes?"

"Of course," responded George, but a tiny seed of doubt had crept in. It would be a sad day, a sad day indeed when Silly Little Goose found the power of flight, joined a flock of migrating geese and flew away to parts unknown.

The gosling began to squirm and George leaned over and placed the cute little bird on the floor. It immediately began playing with George's pant leg, biting and tugging at it. George laughed. It felt good to laugh. It had been a while since he could remember laughing.

"Has it eaten?"

George acted as though he was surprised by the question and responded, "It seemed so content tucked inside my shirt—I never considered—bet it is hungry and probably thirsty too."

"What do geese eat besides grain?"

"Don't know, but I'll bet it would eat chick starter like baby chickens do. Don't we still have a sack somewhere?"

"I'll go get it," said Donna. She went outside to the chicken coop and returned with a partial bag of chick starter and two jar lids. George poured feed into one of the lids and placed it on the floor. Silly Little Goose ignored it. Donna got a glass of water and George poured water in the second jar lid and placed that on the floor near the feed. Silly Little Goose ignored that too. Although the gosling had the instinct to peck its way out of the egg, it apparently did not come into the world with the natural instinct to eat or drink. The baby would have to be taught.

George slipped off the chair and onto his knees. He reached a hand toward the feed and tapped at the lid with an index finger. He swirled the feed with his finger and tapped some more. Silly Little Goose moved clumsily toward the jar lid on its big webbed feet—feet so large they looked like oversized clown shoes—and lumbered to where George's finger was tapping. Silly Little Goose responded, putting its beak in the finely ground brown feed and gobbling the contents. Lifting its head back and elongating its neck, Silly Little Goose swallowed. George tapped a finger in the water and Silly Little Goose drank.

After eating and drinking, Silly Little Goose wiggled its tail and promptly pooped a messy stream. Donna hurried to the kitchen for paper towels. Oblivious to the situation, Silly Little Goose calmly went to George and lay beside him. George reached down, picked up the gosling and tucked it inside his shirt and under his chin. George returned to his chair and the gosling began squirming down George's left sleeve. It went inching its way to the wrist and with no place to go it panicked. Silly Little Goose wiggled, writhed and kicked with its feet. The sharp nails on the ends of the toes scratched George and he let out a little yelp, unbuttoned his sleeve and freed Silly Little Goose.

After George and Donna had finished dinner, and after the many times George had fished Silly Little Goose from his shirt sleeve, George asked Donna, "Think the little bird would like to swim?"

Donna filled the sink with water, tepid to the touch, and covered the drain board with a towel. When Silly Little Goose was placed in the water it immediately became active and animated, floating on the surface and dipping its head underwater, diving with its little black webbed feet wildly thrashing water and air. The gosling was so enthusiastic, so spirited and energetic that all George and Donna could do was to watch and be entertained by the antics of Silly Little Goose. After slopping water all over the counter and floor, the cute fuzzy bird stood on the towel on the counter and preened, cocking its spindly neck and using its beak to pull at downy yellow breast fuzz and reaching all the way back to make sure the budding fuzz near its tail was correctly in place.

Donna asked George, "What are we going to do with Silly Little Goose? It's not going to sleep in our bed."

"Got it figured out," said George confidently. He tucked a towel in a cardboard box, placed Silly Little Goose on the towel and covered the bird with one of his flannel shirts. The box was placed beside the bed, and after a couple of satisfied cheeps, the gosling settled in and slept through the night without making another sound.

*****

With a new day barely breaking, George was awakened to a racket of disturbing cheeps and peeps. He looked over the side of the bed and there was the gosling, standing on tiptoes, fluttering stubby wings and trying to wrestle its way up and out of the cardboard box. Silly Little Goose was demanding food, water and to be cuddled.

George reached down and scooped up the gosling, bringing the ball of yellow down to the warm hollow at the base of his neck. When he looked, it seemed to George as if Silly Little Goose was smiling and had a gleam of happiness in its eyes.

Later, as Donna was getting ready for work, the gosling became fidgety and George got up, laid an open newspaper on the floor and set down the jar lids of food and water, tapping once again to encourage Silly Little Goose to eat and drink.

George began a new daily routine that was centered on the gosling and its demands. George took Silly Little Goose for walks outside, a place George had not allowed himself to wander in the past several weeks. It was springtime. The air was ripe with the pungent smells of evergreens and the sweetness of growing grasses and warm soil. Watching his surroundings like a wary mother hen, George was alert to the myriad of predators that posed a threat to a gosling, especially those that flew—eagles, hawks and falcons. He searched the sky and eyed the bushes at the edge of the yard. Silly Little Goose pecked at the grasses, picked up little sticks with its beak, and was completely oblivious to the surroundings, to the dangers that lurked there. The bird followed George like he was the Pied Piper.

*****

Over the course of the next few days, it became obvious the cardboard box could not restrain the energetic bird for very much longer. Donna came home from work with a solution. She had stopped at a thrift store and purchased a baby playpen with netting on the sides. Silly Little Goose could have feed and water, room to roam and yet its messes were confined. When he went to bed, George set the playpen in the spare bedroom and in the morning the *peeps* and *cheeps* did not awaken him at the break of day. In George's estimation, having a wild goose for a pet was working out perfectly.

*****

Mature male and female Canada geese are colored similarly, with black heads and necks and broad white cheek patches extending from the throat to the rear of the eyes. The breast, abdomen and flanks range from pale gray to a dark chocolate brown, either blending into the black neck or being separated from it by a white collar. The backs and shoulders are dark brown, or black, and a U-shaped white band defines the rump. The bill, legs and feet are black. Females are usually smaller than the males among the seven recognized subspecies of

Canada geese, often collectively referred to as "honkers" because of their distinctive calls.

In flight, Canada geese form a V-shaped pattern that allows each trailing bird to receive lift from the wingtip vortex of the bird in front of it, saving energy and greatly extending the range of a flock of birds over a single bird flying alone. During flight, as the lead goose tires, it drops back in the formation and a new leader moves into position.

In the wilds, Canada geese graze on berries, grasses and grains; and swimming on lakes, rivers and streams they reach underwater with their long necks to feed on submerged aquatic vegetation. Geese typically mate for life and a breeding pair exhibits strong family bonds, returning to their natal homes year after year. The nest is a bowl-shaped depression approximately 18 inches in diameter and lined with an assortment of twigs, grasses, leaves, and goose down. The location of nests can vary widely; from shorelines to islands, cattails, clumps of willows and even haystacks and the exposed tops of rocks. An adult pair usually begins nesting at three years of age. The female typically lays five or six eggs in March, April or May and incubates the eggs for about a month, leaving the nest briefly to feed while the male (gander) stands guard over the nest. When the young, called goslings, have hatched they develop quickly and can walk, swim and feed within a day. The family groups generally stay together until the following breeding season.

Canada geese raise only one clutch per year and mortality is high because of predators: humans, coyotes, raccoons, skunks, bobcats, and foxes, as well as gulls, eagles, hawks, crows, ravens, and magpies. The average lifespan for a migrating goose is about 12 years, but in captivity they typically live twice that long.

Once a year, usually in June and July, adult Canada geese molt, replacing worn or lost feathers with new feathers. At this stage, none of the geese can fly—the adults because they are growing new feathers and the young because they have not yet grown flight feathers. During this time, geese are most susceptible to predators and they generally stay near lakes or rivers so they have avenues of easy escape. By the height of summer, geese are flying and by late fall they begin to form into large flocks.

The Western Canada goose (Branta canadensis moffitti) communicates in a variety of ways. A goose is on alert when its neck is extended vertically and its head is in a horizontal position. When a goose is in a conflict situation it coils its neck back, lowers its head and points its beak toward the opposition. It will pump its head if the threat persists. A goose shows a wide range of emotions by preening, extending its neck and lifting its head, and making a variety of sounds including hisses, honks, toots and noises that can be high pitched or low and guttural. The gander will usually have a deeper voice than its mate.

For a goose to migrate, it must be taught the flight paths by its parents, flying north to the tundra of the Far North in the spring and south to warmer climates in Mexico during late fall. Non-migrating geese (often called resident geese) stay year-round in the vicinity where they were hatched. This population is expanding because an urban environment has few predators, hunting is prohibited, and there is usually a dependable supply of food nearby. Canada geese are protected under federal and state law and a hunting license and open season are required to hunt them.

*****

Silly Little Goose soon outgrew its nickname. It was no longer so silly, and certainly no longer little. The goose had become a teenager, sprouting real feathers, coarse and rough. It had become all legs and feet and awkwardness, and its voice no longer chirped like the laughter of a baby. The voice that now issued forth from the long neck was somewhere between an unpleasant honk and a toot. George began to call Silly Little Goose by a new name, *Tootie*.

If Tootie lost sight of George, the goose squawked, flapped its undersized wings and carried on until George reappeared. When the goose saw George it tooted happily, went directly to him and rubbed its long neck against his pant legs. If George bent over or got on one knee, Tootie would preen George's hair.

*****

George did not have the strength or physical stamina necessary to be Tootie's full-time companion and guardian. The bird had become too demanding and consumed too much time. George decided to build an outdoor pen for Tootie: a bird run enclosed in wire that would allow for maximum protection against predators, whether those predators crawled, slinked or swooped from the sky. He asked Donna to stop at the feed store on the way home and pick up a roll of chicken wire, clips and metal T-posts. His plan was to build a four-by-six foot pen. With a tarp slung over one end, Tootie would have maximum protection as well as adequate shade.

As they worked on the pen, Donna observed that George was no longer the same man he had been in the weeks after his diagnosis with cardiomyopathy. Back then it was as though a death sentence had been handed down. George had readily accepted the finality of his disease and was content to lie in bed; afraid to die, afraid to live, afraid to even move. But here he was, wielding a heavy post driver to set the metal T-posts, and stretching, cutting and clipping the chicken wire. When the pen was completed, the door was opened and food and water were set inside. To complete the goose pen, Donna had purchased a small plastic child's wading pool and George and Donna took turns packing buckets of water so Tootie would have a place to swim. They placed Tootie in the new environment and the goose responded by immediately trying out the pool, splashing, and walking around inspecting the interior of the enclosure.

George talked baby talk, "Tootie like the new home."

"Tootie is a happy bird," encouraged Donna.

Tootie returned to swimming and George and Donna went about gathering the tools. They were packing them to the shop and had just stepped out of sight of the pen, when there was a terrible commotion. They raced back to find Tootie squawking, leaping in the air, beating wings, thrashing about and trying to escape. George threw open the door and crawled inside. He gathered Tootie in his arms and the goose quieted. Blood was dripping off Tootie's beak and the skin along the side of its head was rubbed raw and bleeding. Donna ran inside and returned with a wet washrag. George used the washrag to dab away the blood.

*****

Bud and Judy Miller were George and Donna's lifelong friends. Bud called and asked if George and Donna were up for visitors. George assured him they were, but warned they had acquired an "unusual" pet.

Tootie had taken over the spare bedroom and overnight visitors posed a problem. George and Donna moved the nighttime playpen into their bedroom, and the spare room was returned to a guest bedroom.

Bud, a very energetic man who tended to form an opinion quickly, and never hesitated to voice that opinion, immediately fell in love with Tootie. Yet that love affair was not always reciprocated. Any time Bud stood too close to George or Donna,

Tootie intervened, pecking at Bud's pant leg until he moved back a step or two.

"Where is the pool for Tootie to swim in?" asked Bud.

"I've read up on that," said George. "It's an old wives' tale that geese need water to eat or to swim in. They clean themselves by preening."

"Look at those feet. Are they webbed?"

"Well, yes."

"They're webbed for a reason. This goose needs a pool— something bigger than a baby pool—and by God we're going to build a *real* pool."

The pool Bud envisioned was simple to build, requiring two-by-sixes, a handful of nails and heavy black plastic. When it was finished, a hose was uncoiled to fill it. The pool was long and narrow and when George lifted Tootie into the water for that first swim, Tootie splashed, swam and played with wild glee. The two men were amazed at the way Tootie clowned, but there was one problem. There was no way for the goose to get in the pool or to exit without human help. That problem was quickly overcome. The two men installed a ramp with board cleats leading up to the pool and another inside the pool. Tootie learned fast and George praised his pet and bragged to his friend, "Tootie is a real smart goose."

After Tootie swam for a few minutes, the goose climbed onto the ramp and stood preening until the yellow down and the emerging chocolate brown feathers glowed with good health. Sometimes the goose flapped its wings too enthusiastically, lost its balance and tumbled back into the pool.

"Back on the farm, when I was a kid, we used to raise geese. We sold eggs in town and sold the birds at Thanksgiving," announced Bud. "I got so I could identify the sex of a goose and be right 99 times out of 100. Watching Tootie, I'd say without a doubt, you got yourself a female."

"What makes you think so?" asked George.

"A gander, even from an early age, stands tall, trying to show dominance. Watch Tootie. She stays low and extends her neck; definitely a show of submissiveness. And another thing—her voice—a male tries to show off. He will boast loudly, like a young man who has had too much to drink. Tootie is quiet unless she has something to say. Yep, you got yourself a girl goose."

*****

Bud and Judy stayed an extra day so Bud could help screen the back porch for Tootie. The room gave the growing goose ample space in a protected environment. After the friends departed, all George had to do to get Tootie excited was to call, "Where's Uncle Bud? Where's Uncle Bud?" and Tootie went looking, searching for Bud, chirping and occasionally emitting a boisterous adolescent honk. This noise always came as a shocking surprise to Tootie, and she was never quite sure from what source that unfamiliar voice might have emanated.

The spare bedroom once again became Tootie's room. The bed was dismantled and leaned against the wall. Old sheets— Donna bought sheets at a thrift shop—were placed on the floor as well as a thin pile of newspapers in one corner. Tootie made few messes in her room, and when a mess was made, it was generally confined to the newspapers. It was as if the goose had trained herself to become housebroken.

The daily routine revolved around Donna getting up and going to work, while George took Tootie outside for her morning business and the opportunity to stretch and move around in the back yard. George always stood watch, making sure no predators were in the vicinity. If hawks or eagles were flying, George hustled his pet inside. After Donna was gone, George placed a towel on the kitchen table and lifted Tootie onto it. He took a seat while Tootie dutifully preened his hair, using beak and quick head movement to comb through his salt-and-pepper hair. In the wild, the goslings take turns preening each other, and as they grow into adults, they preen themselves and their mates. Tootie took absolute delight from the sessions. She was showing she had chosen George to be her mate—bonded together for life.

*****

With summer in full swing, and Tootie having outgrown her small pool—and even the larger pool Bud had helped build—George and Donna decided to build a goose friendly water feature in their back yard. They went to a home and garden center in Klamath Falls and purchased a pond kit. They came home, picked out a spot in the back yard, and went to work busting sod and shoveling dirt. Donna was amazed at George. He had not exhibited so much stamina in a long, long time.

While they worked, Tootie was allowed outside. She was very interested in what Daddy and Mommy were doing and scrutinized each shovel of dirt. If she found a bug or a worm, she quickly devoured them. George continued working at his pace—not fast, just steadily—taking short breaks when he needed to. He was conscious of his fragile physical condition and tried not to push himself to the point of fatigue.

According to the directions for the water feature, the hole for placement of the kit was to be six feet wide, eight feet long and two feet deep, with a gently tapered slope from the sides to the flat bottom. As Tootie was exploring she stepped too close to the edge of the hole and fell in. Rather than lift the goose out, George allowed her to remain there. It was a hot day and George brought out Tootie's bowl of water and set it in the bottom of the hole. It was obvious the bird was thirsty, and as she dunked her head in and out of the water a spill was created. It was then George made an important discovery. Tootie, using her oversized webbed feet, stomped up and down creating more mud, and then she picked up the mud with her beak and sifted the mud with water from the water pan.

"Look at Tootie stomp those swampers," called George with a laugh. He grew pensive. "Geese love mud. I never knew. How many times has that silly goose wanted me to go out, demanded to go out, and she spent all the time pecking around in the grass. I'll just bet she was after grit. That's how ducks, geese and chickens digest their food. We need to buy a bag of grit."

When the digging was finished, George and Donna put away their shovels and stretched the kit liner and then the black plastic tarp over the hole. The last step was to fill the pond with a garden hose. Before water had even covered the bottom of the pool, Tootie used the plastic like a slide and went skating down the incline on her feet and rear end. George and Donna sat on the lawn and shared in Tootie's happiness as afternoon faded and light bled from the day.

"What a hoot," said Donna, nodding in the direction of the pool. The goose was diving under the water, tail sticking up like a flag waving in a parade.

The pond was full and George turned off the hose. Tootie stepped from the water onto the lawn and began feeding. From somewhere in the growing darkness, a coyote yipped and George swiftly scooped up Tootie, telling her, "Time to go in."

*****

Children often get attached to a particular blanket. They insist on having that blanket when sleeping and drag it around like a toy during the day. Tootie was the same as a child. She had one particular blanket, pink in color with fringe, and she loved to have that blanket pulled partially over her back. She delighted in preening the fringe. To get Tootie excited all

34

George had to ask was, "Where's your blanky? Where's your blanky?" Tootie stood on her toes, wiggled her neck, opened her beak wide and honked. She kept up the racket until the blanket was produced, and then she dutifully preened the fringe until finally dipping a shoulder under a corner of the blanket and napping.

*****

Tootie was maturing fast. Pin feathers and then real feathers had replaced the cute yellow fuzz. The primary flight feathers were growing in, and when she ran to catch up to George, she now spread her wings and flapped them. At first George tried to discourage this behavior. He had read that flight is a learned behavior and that geese will stay in familiar surroundings if they are not taught the fine art of flying.

Despite George's reservations about teaching Tootie to fly, she had a mind of her own. On walks she purposely put distance between herself and George and then hurried to catch up, her feet skimming along the ground taking big steps while frantically beating her wings and honking loudly.

One day Tootie threw herself into flight. She weaved between pine trees, squawked noisily and seemed to be calling, "Look at me! Look at me!" A hundred yards downhill she landed in a clumsy heap of feathers, legs and dust. It was just short of a crash landing. She took no notice, turned to face George and bobbed her head up and down, demanding to know if he had witnessed her monumental moment of liftoff and experimental flight.

For a long moment George did not move. He was unsure how he should react, and then at last his hands came together and he applauded. Walking back to the house, George was remembering the saying, *If you love something, set it free*. He was not ready for that. He did not want Tootie to fly away.

35

And now his heart began to flutter and race. All at once he felt dizzy, unsteady on his feet and sick to his stomach. He could not maintain an upright position and slowly sank to one knee. His head was bowed as if in prayer and it felt to him as if his damaged heart was going to race away. He clenched his jaw against the pain. Tootie came close to George and laid her head on George's shoulder until the event passed.

*****

George told Donna about Tootie's flight and, of course, Donna immediately wanted to know, "Does that mean she's going to fly away and leave us?"

"Not necessarily. But if she does, then that is what happens."

"Maybe we should clip her wings so she can't fly."

"That would be making the decision for her. I think Tootie is the one that has to make that decision."

It was not until later that evening that George was honest with Donna and told her of the *episode* with his heart. He admitted he had been scared. Donna insisted they make an appointment with Doctor George Kubac, George's cardiologist, and the doctor who had diagnosed George's cardiomyopathy.

*****

After Doctor Kubac listened to George tell the story of Tootie and her first flight, and about the symptoms of his *episode,* he concluded stress may have been a contributing factor. The doctor explained that dilated cardiomyopathy is often passed from one generation to the next. "Luck of the draw," as Doctor Kubac put it. He clarified that dilated cardiomyopathy develops when the heart ventricles enlarge and weaken. The condition usually starts in the left ventricle and can affect the right ventricle too. The weakened chambers of the heart do not pump effectively, causing the heart muscle to work harder. Over time, the heart loses the ability to pump blood effectively. This leads to heart valve disease, irregular heart rate, and blood clots in the heart which might result in a stroke and heart failure.

During his latest *episode* George had experienced faintness, difficulty breathing, and arrhythmia. Although the symptoms diminished in time, it was obvious to Doctor Kubac that George's disease was escalating. Since the *episode*, George had felt absolutely exhausted and he suffered with swollen legs and ankles.

"Chances are," said Doctor Kubac, "as your disease progresses, the frequency of your attacks will increase. As the heart weakens, healthy muscle will be replaced by scar tissue. The heart will be less efficient and have difficulty maintaining a normal electrical rhythm. As you know, this can lead to heart failure. You are currently experiencing fluid build up and you are extremely fatigued. These are classic symptoms of heart failure."

Doctor Kubac suggested that George and Donna might want to consider looking for a home closer to the hospital in Klamath Falls. Where they were living required an hour and a half drive, and in bad weather, with the wind blowing and snow drifting, the drive might take twice that long, if they could make it at all.

"Won't the stress of moving make it worse?" asked George. But he was not thinking of himself and the complications he was facing. He was thinking about Tootie and trying to find a place close to town, but far enough out that Tootie could spread her wings and fly.

"Best if you do it now," said the doctor, "rather than wait until you are in a crisis situation."

*****

It was not going to be an easy task for George and Donna to find a new home, especially with acreage that they could afford. But everything fell into place as if divine intervention was lending a hand. George learned of a manufactured home at the edge of a golf course that had been repossessed by a bank. The bank thought the property would be easier to sell as a building site and was willing to sell the manufactured home for next to nothing. George made an offer and the bank accepted.

The next hurdle was finding a parcel of land within 30 miles of Klamath Falls and not too close to neighbors. They found the perfect location 10 miles north of the small community of Bonanza, Oregon. The three forested acres—pine, cedar and juniper, along with sagebrush and buck brush—sloped downward from a hill to a snow melt reservoir. There were neighbors, but none too close. George and Donna used their life savings and purchased the property.

With friends helping, work on the site began. A well was drilled, septic tank and drain field installed, foundation poured and the manufactured home was brought 60 miles to the site. A back deck was added, as well as an enclosed room for Tootie, complete with her private pond. A fenced back yard would keep Tootie safe from four-legged predators.

Moving day arrived and George was worried how Tootie might react. She had never been in a car. Would she be frightened? And what about flying? She was full grown and flying on a regular basis now. When George turned her loose at the new house, would she become confused and fly away? Would she try to return to the only home she had ever known?

George loaded a large dog carrier in the front seat of the pickup with the door facing the driver. He loaded Tootie in the carrier. Not liking to be confined she squawked, flapped her wings, repeatedly bashed her head against the top of the dog carrier and bit at the wire. George kept talking to her, reassuring her that they were going to a new home and all was going to be fine. As they drove, Tootie stood spraddle-legged, beak open wide, making a hissing sound. The road was windy, and after a long hour of travel, they arrived at their new home. George parked and transported the cage, and Tootie, to her special room on the back porch. George opened the cage door and stepped back.

Tootie pouted and stayed inside the cage for one long moment, and then an enormous webbed foot cautiously tested the opening. She stepped into view, shook herself like she did when she rolled in the dust, made a low guttural noise and walked directly to the pool and settled herself in the water. She bobbed her head up and down several times and turned to face George. It almost seemed to George as if Tootie spoke and said, "Okay. I can live with this."

George opened the door from the back porch and coaxed her inside. Boxes were stacked everywhere, but the same sofa was there and the same television was there. Tootie climbed up on the sofa like she had always done and watched television. George told her, "See, nothing has changed."

Tootie was given a tour of the house. In fact, it was Tootie that led the way. She twisted her head this way and that, long neck coiling and uncoiling. She looked everything over. Occasionally she gave a little nod or made a sound.

Tootie waddled down the hall, chattering away as she stepped around boxes and into George and Donna's bedroom. She pulled at the familiar bedspread with her beak and went down the hall to the next bedroom. This would be Tootie's room. There was plastic on the floor, a fleece dog bed, a slim pile of newspapers and a dish of food and a dish of water. She drank and took a few bites of the cracked corn. The room apparently met Tootie's approval and she marched on down the hall, hopped up on the sofa and went back to watching television.

*****

At the Heart Clinic in Klamath Falls, Doctor Kubac assured George, "You are doing well right now." George grinned at the good news but the grin was short-lived and disappeared entirely as the doctor continued. "From this point forward your health will decline rather rapidly. Nothing can be done to stop, or even slow, the steady progression of the disease. We are nearing the point where I will not be able to do anything more to help you. When it gets bad, and it will get bad, how far do you wish to proceed? Do you want to consider a heart transplant?"

"I have too many things I want to do. If I need a new heart then, sure, I'm willing to go the distance."

"I thought that would be your decision," said Doctor Kubac. "Your next step is to travel to Portland, to Oregon Health and Science University (OHSU) where a complete cardiac evaluation will be performed. I've already made the arrangements."

*****

At OHSU George underwent very intensive testing and evaluations that lasted more than a week. At the conclusion, the team of doctors informed George that although he was an excellent candidate for a heart transplant, his condition had not reached that critical point where his life was in serious jeopardy. But they warned, George's heart would continue to deteriorate, and in the near future he would reach that critical point. However, he was not there yet.

On their way home from Portland, George and Donna discussed their future. Donna was very concerned that George's condition could—*would*—dramatically worsen. If he went into cardiac arrest and died before he got a heart transplant, she would lose the love of her life and be left alone.

*****

Bud and Judy Miller had driven north from their home in Arizona to care for Tootie while George and Donna visited OHSU in Portland. They stayed on after George and Donna returned to help complete several projects. They went to work on the back yard; leveling, raking and getting the soil ready for grass seed. Tootie was there, shaking her head and talking, offering advice and stating her opinion about the work that was being done. At those times when, in Tootie's estimation, Bud was working too close to George she pecked at Bud's pant leg and hissed at him. She was even more protective of George now than she had ever been.

The lawn was planted and the crew went to work building a shop. Bud was handy with construction and did most of the heavy work as forms were set, concrete poured and stud walls lifted into place. It was looking like they might finish the shop before winter set in.

One afternoon George went to the house to get soft drinks. When he returned he found Bud sitting on the top of a ladder in the middle of the unfinished shop. Tootie was guarding the base, wings outstretched. She was very agitated. George chuckled and remarked, "Why are you so afraid, Bud? She's a goose, not a grizzly bear."

*****

41

The shop was finished and Bud and Judy returned to Arizona. George could now relax and spend time with Tootie. They went on walks together and George sat and watched Tootie search through the shoots of grass in the new lawn. If she found a bug, she seized it in her beak, twisted her neck and flipped the bug. If she came across a grasshopper she tilted her head, raised her lower eyelids to make her eyes appear to almost bulge, and gave the hopper the *evil eye*.

The porch—Tootie's room—had been fixed to her liking. The screened windows had been wrapped in heavy plastic, the inside pond was heated and there was a fleece-lined dog bed where Tootie could nap. After taking a swim, Tootie liked to stand under the radiant rays of the heat lamp and preen. Later, when the weather turned cold, Tootie would move to the spare bedroom that had been converted into a goose sanctuary.

In the evenings, while Donna cooked, Tootie often got off the sofa where she sat with George, and wandered into the kitchen to beg for food. If Donna ignored her, Tootie took hold of Donna's shirt tails and tugged until Donna gave her scraps of food—cookies, crackers and bread, even chicken—but Tootie's favorite treat was yogurt, which Donna fed her on a spoon.

Before dark, Tootie went outside to do her business and take a quick flight, usually to the roof. To coax her down, George or Donna used a piece of bread or a cookie crumb. After eating the tidbit, Tootie enjoyed a swim, unless frogs were in the water-feature pond. She did not like their croaking and shook her head and refused to go anywhere near the water.

After the first snowstorm of the year, George spent the majority of his time in the new shop, organizing tools, and on the days he had energy, building shelves and cabinets. When these chores were completed he started working on his '37 Chevy. As he worked, Tootie was his constant companion.

Because of the deterioration of his heart, George was given a full disability from the Social Security Administration. That additional income allowed Donna to quit her job and devote herself to being George's full-time caregiver.

*****

Donna had always considered herself a *creative* person. Over the years she had dabbled with a number of hobbies, including painting. As a child she had loved to draw and her teachers and her mother had encouraged her, telling her she had real talent. Now she had time to pursue art. She took several art classes in Klamath Falls and chose to paint with acrylics because it was a medium that was easy to work with, and not as difficult as watercolors or as messy as oils. Her talents bloomed. Most of the subjects of her paintings were what she saw in the natural environment around her rural home; landscapes, birds and animals. Like most artists, Donna painted on stretched canvas, but she found it more rewarding to paint on something she found; an unusual stick, a board, even leaves, and then one day she was looking at Tootie and thought, "Why not paint on a feather?"

When Donna went on hikes she was constantly on the lookout for feathers. She painted birds and scenes of wildlife on these feathers. She gave her artwork away as gifts. Those gifts led to commissioned works. She did not know what to charge her customers and simply asked people to pay what they thought a particular piece of art was worth. Most clients paid more than Donna would ever have dreamed to charge. Her art became collectible and she was asked to sell her work at art shows in the Klamath Basin. Several galleries contacted her, wanting her to exhibit her work. Whenever Donna spoke to people in the art community, she always made mention that her inspiration for painting on feathers came from Tootie, a family pet, a Canada goose. The novelty of a tame goose piqued everyone's interest and gave Donna the confidence to relate the story about finding the egg, her husband stricken with cardiomyopathy hatching the egg, and details of their unusual pet.

*****

The story of the painter and the pet goose made the rounds and Lee Juillerat, a feature writer for the Klamath Falls *Herald and News* newspaper, contacted Donna and asked if he could come out and interview her for a story. Donna asked in astonishment, "You want to write a story about me?"

In addition to his writing skills, Lee was also an accomplished photographer. The day he arrived to do the interview with Donna, he was armed with a notepad and a camera. Tootie, as was her midmorning custom, was perched on the roof and was the first to notice a car coming up the driveway. She honked loudly.

George and Donna stepped outside to greet Lee. They shook hands and Donna remarked, "Tootie is going to be jealous." From the rooftop, Tootie squawked.

"Come to Daddy," encouraged George.

"That's Tootie," Donna informed Lee, "our pet Canada goose."

As if on cue, and with a thunderous beating of wings and shrill calls, Tootie lifted from the peak of the roof and swooped down, landing beside George, wrapping her outstretched wings around him to alert the intruder that George belonged to her, and warning Lee to stay well enough away.

Lee immediately began shooting photographs and busily jotting notes. George suggested they step around to the back yard so Tootie could play, and they could visit. Tootie was the animated star of the show. She slid into her pool, flapped her wings and ducked her head underwater until only her tail feathers were exposed. George had placed one of his old tennis shoes in the pond for Tootie to play with and she chased it around the pool while Lee shot more photographs.

"Go bring Daddy your hat," George baby talked and Tootie dutifully found the baseball hat and brought it to George.

"She understands what I'm saying. Watch this."

George flipped the hat and it sailed like a Frisbee. "Go get it," encouraged George and Tootie playfully chased the hat; wings widespread and mouth agape, making huffing sounds. When she got to the hat she pecked at it until George picked up the hat and casually tossed it in a different direction. The game continued for a few minutes, until George tired and Tootie decided that if Goose Daddy wasn't going to play with her anymore, she would fly to the roof and sulk. Lee wanted to shoot photographs of Tootie flying. George enticed her down with a cracker and Lee got the perfect photo with Tootie seemingly flying straight into the lens.

The story came out as a three-page spread. On the opening page was a large photo of George and Tootie. Her neck was elegantly curved and George was kissing the top of her head. The headline read, "House Goose" and there was a quote attributed to Donna, "Canada geese are social, loving and very interesting. Our Tootie knows words. She is very sweet.... I don't think she knows she's a goose."

The inside two pages featured more photographs of George and Tootie and some of Donna's artwork painted on goose feathers. Donna was again quoted, "Painting on feathers is the best canvas in the world. They aren't as delicate as you might imagine. I make sure that each image tells a story. For me it is personal, and fun."

George was quoted in the article as saying, "Tootie is free to fly away—but I hope she won't—and she is constantly on watch for eagles and hawks. When Canada geese pass over the house she will cock her head and listen, but then she goes back to eating."

What George never mentioned was his fear the first time that a long V of Canada geese passed over the house. Tootie was on the rooftop and she called to them. The birds overhead answered. One bird—George figured it had to have been a male looking for a mate—dropped out of the formation and circled back. He called to Tootie with a forlorn honk. Her answer was short and deliberate. The male hurried away to rejoin the formation. Tootie flew off the roof to be with George. And when she landed at his feet, George realized he had been holding his breath in fear that Tootie would fly away. He petted Tootie and loved her and told her how important she was and how thankful he was to have her in his life.

Tootie became an instant celebrity in the Klamath Basin, and when Donna went to art shows she proudly displayed the *Herald and News* story in an attractive frame. Her artwork sold like never before. It seemed as though everyone wanted one of Tootie's feathers with a painting of her likeness. And on shopping trips, George was stopped in stores and asked, "Are you Goose Daddy?" and he proudly answered he was. He was asked all sorts of questions about Tootie. So many people were interested in Tootie and the story that George told Donna, "I wish Tootie liked to travel. I could write a book and we could hit the road and make a million bucks."

*****

Winter reluctantly gave way to spring and George wanted to finish fencing the three and a half acres and put in an underground sprinkler system so they could water the lawn without having to drag a hose around. But he was too tired to tackle any of the projects. He was tired all the time. At his regular checkup, Doctor Kubac conducted a battery of tests including the very invasive MUGA test where a tiny camera is directed to the heart to test the *ejection fraction*, a measurement of the percentage of blood squeezed from the heart each time the heart contracted. In a healthy heart the ejection fraction should be 70 percent or higher, but George's ejection fraction was operating at less than 20 percent. Doctor Kubac informed George it was now necessary for him to be fitted with a defibrillator pacemaker. The device would be tucked under his skin near his collarbone and was designed to regulate heart rate and hopefully stop any of what the doctor referred to as "sudden death events."

"We don't want any of those," joked George. "At least I don't."

Before that procedure could be performed, at home in the middle of the night, George woke up and knew something was terribly wrong. Donna rushed him to the hospital emergency room in Klamath Falls where it was discovered George's blood pressure had dropped to a dangerously low level. His heart was barely pumping enough blood to keep him alive and this, in turn, was causing his organs—in particular his liver—to shut down. George was stabilized and fitted with a pacemaker. When he was informed he had almost died he responded, "I don't have time to be sick. I've got too many things to do."

*****

George knew his name would soon be placed on the heart transplant list. In his mind, and complicating the inevitability of that action, were the many costs associated with having the heart transplant operation and the financial effects of living on anti-rejection medication for the remainder of his life. Following through with the transplant was not an easy decision for George to make. There was nothing easy about it.

Insurance would only cover part of the immediate and long-term costs. George did not want to saddle Donna with debt. He thought maybe he should just play the cards God had dealt him. That way, when he died, Donna would have the house and land, their savings and his life insurance policy. She was a relatively young woman, an accomplished artist, and after he was gone she could find someone to be her companion. This is what George was thinking, but when he tried to express this to Donna, she refused to listen. She said, "You are going to get a new heart and everything will work out. I just know it."

Summer passed and the nights became longer, the air crisp and clear. George went right on living. He had learned to accept what he could not change, and yet he felt an inner awkwardness, as if *he* was somehow personally responsible for his medical condition. He hated the obvious fact that he could do less and less, and that Donna had to pick up the slack and constantly do more and more. In the next few weeks the cottonwood trees surrounding the runoff lake would turn colors, from green to gold, and begin to lose their grip on summer. For George, he would watch the subtle changes, and the fretful days of his existence would spin from one uneventful day into the next.

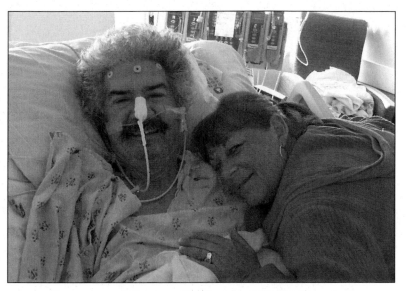

George and Donna Hooker at OHSU Hospital

Chapter Three

George, with Donna at his side, walked into Oregon Health Science University Hospital. They moved slowly. George was only capable of moving slowly. His heart was not pumping enough blood to feed oxygen to his muscles. As they entered the conference room, the team of doctors George had seen on his initial visit greeted them warmly. They asked about Tootie and whether George had been working on his '37 Chevy. They were like old friends and assured George that after a few days of testing they would recommend a course of action. The words they used were that they felt *the outcome will be very favorable.*

After two days of strenuous testing—poking, prodding and drawing blood and more blood—George and Donna were allowed to return home. They were scheduled to visit Portland in two weeks to go over the test results with the doctors. The nurse cautioned, "Have your affairs in order. You might not be going home."

"I'm going to die?"

The nurse smiled at George. "No, I did not mean it that way. What I was attempting to say was, if your test results show you are a viable candidate for a heart transplant, you will stay here until a donor heart can be located."

With winter just around the corner, the house needed to be winterized. The plow had to be put on the tractor and clear plastic wrapped around the porch windows so Tootie would be warm and comfortable. There were so many things George needed to accomplish. But in actuality George did very little over the next two weeks. His energy level was at an all-time low and he spent the majority of his time sitting with Tootie. She must have noticed how gaunt George had become, the ashen color of his skin, and although she could not verbalize her concern she showed it by sitting with him hour after hour and affectionately laying her head against him, or preening his hair. Arrangements were made in case George was required to make an extended stay in Portland. Donna's sister, Carol, volunteered to housesit and care for Tootie.

George and Donna returned to OHSU where they met with the transplant coordinating nurse. She informed George that based on his test results, the condition of his heart had deteriorated markedly, to the point his name was indeed being placed on the heart transplant list. She said it would take a few days to determine his status, but in the meantime he would be hospitalized and an IV drip administered to ease the burden on his damaged heart.

George was unprepared for the finality of it all, that if he did not receive a donor heart relatively soon, he would die. How could he pay for a prolonged stay in Portland? How could he afford the rejection medication? What about Tootie? She was a handful. Could Carol take care of her—watch over her—keep the same routine that Tootie was accustomed to? If George did not return right away, would Tootie fly away looking for him? Before leaving home, George had promised Carol they would call every day, and each time he did call he asked Carol to tell Tootie that Daddy was getting a new heart and would be home soon.

George was having trouble breathing and sleeping had become nearly impossible. His ejection fraction was lower than ever before, eight percent, and even with the IV constantly dripping medication, his organs were on the verge of failure. He was admitted to the Intensive Care Unit so his liver and kidney functions could be monitored around the clock.

All George could do was lie in the hospital bed and think about losing Donna, his soul mate. To be correct, *she* would lose *him*. The failure of his heart had reached a critical point and now it was a race against time. But how was Donna feeling about all this, questioned George. She must be scared to death, and yet she was putting up a good front. She was his Rock of Gibraltar, refusing to even consider anything negative. She was Miss Super Positive. George had always thought of himself as the tough guy. He could get through this; could get through anything. But as George lay between the sterile hospital sheets he came to fully appreciate Donna. He had faulted her for not preparing herself for the worst case scenario. In her defense, the reason Donna refused to consider the negative was because she was too busy trying to keep it all together. She was doing it all; handling the finances, the housework and cooking, supplementing their income with art shows. The list of what Donna did was endless. But until that moment in the hospital, George had never opened his eyes to the big picture. He had been insensitive to Donna and her feelings. He only had to consider living or dying. Donna was the one wrestling with all the details, and the real possibility of losing the love of her life. George was dependent on Donna, totally dependent on her, and he knew it.

When Donna came to visit he told her all this, there in the hospital as they waited for a new heart, a new beginning. He expressed his gratitude, his admiration, and he told Donna how much he loved her. He cried. She cried. They held each other and cried more. They desperately wanted the chance to have their love continue, for their life together to continue. George told Donna, "We're like a pair of geese. We are mated for life." And that was the highest compliment George could think to bestow on his wife. Donna knew that, and loved him all the more.

*****

Five weeks, five long weeks were endured waiting for a heart. At home Indian summer was turning the aspen and cottonwoods that lined Sprague River the color of hammered copper and shades of burnished yellow. In the Willamette Valley the rainy season had begun. Sunlight filtered through ashen clouds and shone weakly in the windows at OHSU Hospital, falling as a flat, pasty glow. Outside, the predominant smells were of moisture and rotting leaves, but inside, George smelled the reek of cleaning solvents, recycled air and the harsh reality of despair. George felt a panic like a covey of quail exploding from the brush feels panic. He had never been hospitalized— so cooped up for such a long stretch of time—in his entire life. Time dragged. Depression was a steady companion. For George, everything hinged on that tiny glimmer of possibility that a donor heart, a heart compatible with his body, would be located in time.

*****

The heart is the hardest working muscle in the human body and is responsible for pumping blood to the organs and throughout the body. Like any other muscle, the heart can be subject to fatigue, especially if weakened by a cardiovascular disease. When damaged beyond repair, a patient's only option may be a heart transplant. Organ donation is the key to saving the life of a patient.

At any one time, between four and five thousand people in the United States are awaiting heart transplants. The average wait is four months. But of all those waiting, only about two thousand heart transplants are performed in the United States each year.

The establishment of a donor system was developed from the National Organ Transplant Act of 1984, a national organ sharing system to guarantee fairness in the allocation of donated organs. Nationally there are more than 120,000 people waiting for much-needed organs. As these patients and their families hold onto hope, the United Network for Organ Sharing (UNOS) manages the list of those individuals across the country, ensuring that the available donor organs go to those who are best matched and in the most need.

Patients are evaluated by transplant physicians to determine when they should be placed on the waiting list. The rules that govern the waiting list vary by organ. General criteria—a patient's medical urgency, blood, tissue and size match with the donor, time on the waiting list and proximity to the donor—guides the distribution of organs. Factors such as a patient's income, celebrity status, and race or ethnic background play no role in determining allocation of organs.

The country is divided into 11 geographic regions, each served by an organ procurement organization (OPO). With the exception of perfectly-matched kidneys and the most urgent liver patients, first priority goes to patients at transplant hospitals located in the immediate geographical region. The use of local donors has several medical benefits to potential recipients, including less time elapsing during the transplant process, the better chance of a successful outcome. The average wait for donor organs varies greatly, from months to years. Many patients die before a healthy transplantable organ can be obtained.

*****

Donna remained the energetic cheerleader, reassuring George he was going to get that new heart and everything was going to be wonderful. It was only a momentary thing, but at last George was able to penetrate that wall of protection Donna had so carefully constructed around them.

"I know you don't want to hear this, but I have to talk to you. Let me say this," George said, pausing to gather his strength and fill his weak lungs with air. "Straight up . . . if I don't make it, I want you to use my life insurance money to pay off the mortgage on the house. It will be up to you whether you want to live there or sell and move to some place that doesn't have as much upkeep...."

George wanted to keep talking, to tell Donna the many specific things she needed to do in his absence, but she interrupted and did not allow him to finish. She placed a finger on his lips and told him, "Hush that talk. You're gonna get a new heart. I just know you are." And George was too weak, so totally exhausted he could not muster the energy to fight against her unbending will. They would not discuss any dire consequences, the what-ifs. Donna said he was going to get a new heart and by God he was going to get a new heart.

*****

If George had been living on borrowed time before, he was now in debt past his limit. Donna, always the diehard optimist, was also a very practical woman and she placed calls to each of George's three children—Brian, Bruce and Jen. She explained the situation to each, bluntly stating that because of the progression of the heart disease, and despite the best efforts of the medical staff at OHSU to locate a donor heart, their father was dying a lingering death. It had come down to the dire fact that George's longevity was being measured, not in years like most people, but in days and hours. He was hanging onto life by a frayed thread. For once, Donna was brutally honest with herself, and with George's children. She made up her mind, when she talked to the children, she would not cry, and she did not cry.

The children—young adults now—came immediately. They entered the hospital room as a group. Even though Donna had forewarned them, nothing could have prepared them for the actual sight of the sickly husk of a man occupying the bed. Only in the vaguest form did he resemble the dynamo of a man they had known growing up. George was underweight, his cheeks sunken and his skin sallow. He seemed old and wan and all used up. If any of the three was shocked, they hid it well in greeting their father with warmth and love. George responded, saying he wished they were getting together under better circumstances. They laughed and joked and talked about old times. And when George began to tire, which he did rather quickly, the three were ushered from the room.

After they were gone, George wrestled with conflicting emotions. He felt happy that his children—he had seen them infrequently over the years—would take time away from their busy lives to drive all the way to Portland to visit him, but he felt a bittersweet sadness in knowing this might be the last time they were together as a family.

*****

Lunch arrived and George was lifting half of his sandwich—ham and cheese on white bread—to his mouth when a doctor burst into the room and snatched away the sandwich. He even took the tray from the stand. Donna was sitting in a chair beside the bed staring wide-eyed at the doctor's irrational behavior.

"You must be having a really bad day," said George trying to be funny.

The doctor just stood there grinning. He asked George, "How are you feeling?"

"About the same," responded George, "Worried. Hungry. Tired."

"You don't have to worry anymore." The doctor's grin widened until it seemed to encompass his entire face. "We found you a new heart! A 21-year-old heart—an absolutely perfect match."

George felt a sudden sensation of warmth that began in his chest and spread throughout his entire body. It had happened—this amazing news—so sudden it now seemed unreal, beyond any realm of possibility. George tried to form words, to ask questions, to thank the doctor, but no words came his way. He lay in stunned silence. Donna squealed and flung herself onto George's bed. She kept repeating, "You're going to get a new heart!"

George was feeling a weird jumble of relief, elation, and abject fear. The news he was to receive a new heart was like the shiny blade of a harrow cutting through the black soil of gloom, and he could feel the pressure of Donna's body against him and knew how much she loved him.

*****

The process of becoming an organ donor begins when a person applies for a driver's license, or renews a driver's license. The applicant is asked if they wish to become an organ donor, a strictly voluntary program. Other ways to become a donor include contacting a state or national donor organization, or it may be as simple as informing your family that you wish to become a donor.

For a patient, organ donation takes place only after all life-saving measures have been exhausted. A physician, neurosurgeon, or neurologist, declares the patient brain dead. If the patient is a candidate to be an organ donor, a transplant coordinator immediately travels to the hospital to review the patient's chart, meet with the medical team and consult with the national list of patients awaiting transplants maintained by the United Network for Organ Sharing (UNOS) located in Richmond, Virginia. The registry includes medical information about the patient and the length of time the patient has been waiting. The waiting list is constantly changing as new patients are added to the list, and as others are taken off the list due to death, a transplant, or a change in medical status.

The transplant coordinator meets with the family of the donor. Once the family consents to the donation the coordinator calls in a team of surgeons to recover the organs. Each organ recovered is infused with a cooled solution, which flushes the blood and preserves the organ. The organ is measured and evaluated closely and placed in a sterile container that is then packed on ice for transportation to the hospital where the transplant will take place. Due to increased preservation times—up to 72 hours for kidneys and 24 hours for livers—the transplant container will typically be driven to the hospital for transplant. A heart can only be maintained and preserved out of the body for about four hours, and with the element of time so critical, the heart is usually flown to the hospital where a team of transplant surgeons and the recipient are waiting.

*****

The date was October 21, 2008. At 2 p.m. George was directed to take a shower and upon returning to his bed several nurses began prepping him; shaving and scrubbing his skin with red iodine. Even his neck and face were scrubbed. One of the nurses told him he looked like an Indian. A pale blue plastic shower-type cap was pulled over his head and any loose hair was tucked under the elastic band.

A nurse leaned very close to George. It seemed her face was only inches away and she said, "When you wake up from the operation everything around you will seem much different. The room will be dark except for a small amount of light from the monitors. There will be a tube down your throat to help you breathe. Relax and let the machine work for you. Stay calm. Don't worry. Everything will be all right."

Two men arrived and introduced themselves to George as anesthesiologists. They worked simultaneously to place IVs in both of George's arms. The procedure was painless except for a sharp sting when each needle was inserted under the skin and into a vein. Clear liquids from plastic bags began to drip into George's bloodstream, drop by measured drop.

Two surgeons dressed in blue scrubs came into the room. They must have thought George was sedated because one doctor asked the other doctor, "Think he's ready?"

"Without a doubt," said the second doctor. "He's got a kick-ass attitude. He'll do just fine."

"What about his wife? Will she be able to handle this?" asked the first doctor.

"She's even more kickass than he is," laughed the second doctor.

George smiled and opened his eyes. One of the doctors noticed and asked, "You ready for a new heart?"

"Let's get 'er done," responded George. His voice was more harsh than he had intended. Before the surgeons departed, George asked if he could make one small request.

"If it's within my power, sure," said the lead surgeon.

George brought out a photograph he kept with him, a photograph of Tootie. He started to explain, but the surgeon waved his hand and said, "Everyone in the hospital knows Tootie. She's famous."

This made George feel good. "I was wondering if it would be okay if I kept her picture with me during the operation."

"Not a problem," said the doctor.

George was beginning to feel groggy, but he needed to know what he was facing, the details of the operation, and he had presence of mind to ask one of the anesthesiologists, "So, how's this going to work?"

The anesthesiologist answered very matter-of-factly, "Your chest will be opened, the breastbone split, and the team of doctors will prep you to receive your new heart. As soon as the heart arrives, like clockwork, the majority of your diseased heart will be surgically removed, only enough will remain to stitch onto your new heart. The two will grow together, fuse as one, but they will constantly try to reject each other. The new heart will always be considered foreign to your body and for the remainder of your life you will be administered medication to counteract that rejection. Okay?"

George was sleepy. He did not know if he answered the anesthesiologists or not. He slept. For Donna, the long wait was just beginning. George was to become the 516th person to receive a donor heart at OHSU.

George and Donna Hooker

Chapter Four

Donna was sensible, levelheaded and mostly content. She had never been the type of woman to buy self-help books or slip on a pair of leotards and do aerobics to a Grateful Dead tune, or for that matter, a Jane Fonda workout. She was born in San Francisco and grew up a city girl. At an early age she discovered boys and was only 16 when she dropped out of high school and got married. She and her husband had two boys, Kirk and Mark, but the marriage faltered. Perhaps they had gotten married too young, or it might have been that Donna and her husband, a road salesman, simply grew apart. After two decades of marriage they divorced.

George was born in Sacramento, but raised in the country, attending a two-room school in a converted farmhouse. His playground was the rural valley and the Sacramento River.

Hot rods were his first real love, souped-up muscle cars from the '50s and '60s. On Friday and Saturday nights, George and his high school buddies who had cars would cruise K Street in Sacramento; rock-and-roll music blaring from the radios— *Hound Dog, Rock Around the Clock, Heartbreak Hotel, Don't Be Cruel*. George's father was a strict disciplinarian and would not allow his son to have a car, not until he graduated from high school and had full-time employment.

George did graduate—Norte Del Rio High School—and began working for the State of California in a printing plant. He purchased a very practical car, a Nash Rambler, and asked his steady girlfriend, Rita, to be his wife. Over the following two decades George had a variety of jobs: apprentice welder at Mare Island Ship Yard, maintenance for FMC Chemical in a mine two thousand feet underground, welding for the Union Pacific Railroad, and finally as the Building Maintenance Supervisor for the City of Sacramento. He and Rita had three children; two boys, Brian and Bruce, and a daughter, Jen.

George never had the time or inclination to be involved in the hippy movement and the iconic love-ins going on in the nearby Haight-Ashbury district of San Francisco. When the Vietnam War came along, stealing every available young man in the draft, George was safe with a family deferment. He lived the same life as a lot of other Baby Boomers until his marriage disintegrated. Then his life changed drastically. He and Rita tried a trial separation, got back together for a while, but that failed and after an extremely acrimonious parting, George and Rita divorced.

The children were still in high school and they stayed with Rita. George paid alimony and child support and moved into a small apartment. He suddenly had free time on his hands and one day, glancing through the classified ads in the *Sacramento Bee*, he came across a private party selling a 1937 Chevy Master

Deluxe Coupe. That car brought back fond memories to George. His grandmother had driven an automobile of that same make and model. She had taken George for leisurely Sunday drives when he was young. He loved that car. He now thought about all those years, the responsibilities of being a husband and father, and the fact he had never allowed himself the indulgence of either the time or money to start a project car, but now if he were to buy the car being advertised, he could fix it up and finally have that hot rod he had always wanted.

George drove over and took a look at the '37. The owner had purchased the car with the thought of restoring it, but for 25 years it sat in a garage collecting dust. Then a fire nearly destroyed the car; a fire so hot it scorched the black paint, turning it an ugly gunmetal gray, melted the lead connecting the body and fenders, and ruined the safety glass and the interior. George paid the asking price, a thousand bucks, and trailered the damaged car to a buddy's garage where they began working on it every weekend and sometimes after work.

*****

At the time it was introduced to the marketplace, the 1937 Chevrolet Master Deluxe was touted as *The Complete Car, Completely New.* Chevrolet, needing to compete against the Ford Coupe, spent more than 26 million dollars retooling— an astronomical figure by the standards of the day—and the designers came up with what proved to be the forerunner of all muscle cars. The impressive new styling was the work of automotive artist Jules Agramonte and production was spearheaded by General Motors' chief designer, Harley Earl. He later gained fame as the inventor of the Corvette. At the heart of the 1937 Chevrolet Master Deluxe was the *diamond crown speedline*, a trend-setting highlight featuring a body crease that started in the valley between the engine compartment and

RICK STEBER

front fenders and extended across the cowling and onto the doors for a sleek, low profile look. The body was wide and roomy and made entirely of steel, the upholstery had been upgraded, and beneath the hood was a brand new engine with overhead valves, a short stroke and a larger bore. Displacement was increased slightly, to 216.5 cubic inches, with 85 horsepower. The design proved extremely popular and outsold the Ford Coupe with sales of nearly 200,000 units.

*****

George was working on his hot rod at his buddy's garage when he first met the next door neighbor over the adjoining fence. It was Donna. After his failed marriage, George was gun shy about starting a relationship, but he was impressed with Donna. He thought she was pretty. She was fun to talk to and they shared similar interests. They just seemed to hit it off. George invited Donna over to take a look at his project car. He warned that the car was *bare bones,* and when she stepped into the garage, George went into detail about how he was going to modify the '37 and turn it into a hot rod. Donna seemed to share his excitement and even said she could envision how it would turn out. It was probably at that moment—when Donna expressed actual interest in his car—that George found himself beginning to fall in love. They sat side by side on a sawhorse, drinking beer and exchanged stories about the heartbreak of their divorces, about their children, about life. They talked, and talked, and talked.

According to Donna, what impressed her most about George was his witty sense of humor. He made her laugh. George was smitten, and even though he kept flirting with Donna, their relationship progressed as slow as a glacier inching downhill. They became friends, and then best friends. According to George, he knew from the first meeting over the fence that

Donna was his *soul mate*. They were meant for each other. In 1985 they ran off to Lake Tahoe and got married.

They moved to Placerville and built a house. It seemed they had the world by the tail on a downhill pull, and then it all went south. George began losing weight. He drank water to excess and exhaustion became his constant companion. For a go-getter like George, these symptoms were devastating. He went to a doctor who discovered George was suffering from type 2 diabetes. The disease was so advanced the City of Sacramento put George on partial permanent disability. His working days were over.

Three Birds

Jonathan Ashley Thomas Brown

Renate Boronowsky and Jon Brown, age 2

Jon Brown, age 3

Jon Brown, age 12

Jon Brown, age 15

Jonathan Ashley Thomas Brown
(Los Gatos High School graduation photo)

Chapter Five

Jonathan "Jon" Brown was a 21-year-old floppy-haired California no-worries dude with a spirit as wild and free as one of those warm summer breezes blowing in fresh off the vast Pacific Ocean. He was intelligent, curious, and handsome with an original style, and he certainly never took himself too seriously. He had a goofy grin, both disarming and infectious, that he often flashed at friends and the unsuspecting. His physical appearance could be oddly deceiving and rather contradictory; graceful and athletic and at the same time gangly and awkward—all elbows, arms, knees and legs seemingly driving in different directions—like a frisky colt just beginning to grow into his powerful body. Family was extremely important to Jon and he was still living at home, attending community college and taking classes in philosophy, mechanical engineering and computer science. His passions were many and varied and he enjoyed reading and thought someday he just might want to write a novel. He never doubted he could accomplish something of such a magnitude. He was a champion for the underdog, the disenfranchised and the weak of the world. Others were naturally drawn to Jon's beacon of light and among his peers he was known to be a bit of a party boy. He smoked a little weed, drank beer, chased girls and had his fair share of fun. He was known by a variety of names— Jonathan, Jon, Jon-Jon, Johnny—and friends gave him the nickname "Jon-Go" because Jon would be at a party, or just hanging out, and suddenly disappear, prompting someone to ask, "Where'd Jon go?" And that was the way it was. Here one moment, gone the next. Jon-Go.

Jon was an only child. His parents, Jeanne Siggens and Peter Brown, had met at Lifespring, a New Age training session held in San Mateo. They were searching for more fulfillment and happiness in their lives. What they found at that weekend retreat was each other.

Peter was funny and extremely intelligent. He was well-read and well-versed and worked in the Silicon Valley in high tech product marketing. Jeanne worked in the same industry. She had been born in Chippewa Falls, Wisconsin, and had moved with her parents to California in 1972 to begin her freshman year at Carlmont High School. She and Peter married on the last day of December, 1985.

Jonathan Ashley Thomas Brown was born April 29, 1987 in Mountain View, California. During the pregnancy, Peter was not at all sure he was cut out for fatherhood, and although he attended and participated in the Lamaze classes with Jeanne, he remained reticent. The minute Jon was born he changed his tune.

One time, not long after they brought their baby home, Jeanne was in the kitchen fixing dinner and Peter was in the living room holding his son. Jeanne stepped into the living room and found Peter weeping. Instinctively she feared something was wrong, but Peter looked up, smiled and said, "This new life we have been blessed with is just such a wonderful miracle."

Their baby's official name came from a combination of family names as well as Thomas Jefferson, Peter's favorite historical figure. Jon was a sweet baby, but he had a little devilish streak and sometimes when Jeanne was holding him, Jon would butt heads and laugh. As soon as he could crawl, he was exploring. He loved to dig up the dirt in the potted plants, and sometimes he ate the dirt. He discovered the slot in the VCR and his parents never knew what they would find in there: crackers, Cheerios, bits and pieces of sandwiches and even screws and nuts and bolts. Jon was never sick, almost always slept through the night and woke up in a happy mood, calling out, "Ma-ma." If Jeanne did not respond immediately, and free Jon from the confines of his crib, he called louder and louder until she could no longer ignore him.

From kindergarten through the primary grades, the teachers always complimented Jon to his parents, saying he was very bright, creative and artistic, as well as polite and respectful. They said that Jon went out of his way to make new friends, did not tolerate injustice of any kind and if a kid was being picked on, Jon consistently stood up for the underdog. He made friends with kids even if they were not popular or part of the *in* crowd.

Jeanne and Peter divorced when Jon was five, but they continued to live near each other and shared custody of their son. Jon frequently pedaled his bike between the homes of his parents. Both parents were soon remarried and Jon seemed to take all this in stride, at least on the surface he seemed to.

He was a loving and affectionate son to both parents, and to his new stepmother and stepfather.

Jon did well in school. He was athletic and in high school took up surfing in the summer and snowboarding in the winter, but never took any interest in team sports. His focus varied from electronics to philosophy. He went through an extended phase where he volunteered at the Los Gatos Fire Department and his passion seemed to center on fighting fires and serving on an EMT crew. He told friends he wanted to save lives. After graduating from Los Gatos High School, Jon enrolled at Cabrillo College, a community college overlooking Monterey Bay in Aptos, California. He announced his long-range plan was to get his Bachelor of Science degree in engineering and continue on for a Masters Degree in philosophy. His favorite activities included snowboarding, surfing and hiking. He loved exploring in the biologically diverse Santa Cruz Mountains— from the coastal ecosystems of redwood forests to the drought resistant chaparral and manzanita of the high country. He once wrote, "Nature intrigues me. I can't stop myself from going exploring whenever I get the chance. There is something so thrilling about wandering out in the wilderness and coming upon something that you're sure no one else has stumbled onto in some time. You tell people about it and they always want you to take them there."

In 2007, Jon and members of his family attended a *Phil Lesh and Friends* musical concert in Colorado. Phil Lesh, a founding member of the Grateful Dead and the band's bass player, had struck out on his own after the breakup of the band following the death of Jerry Garcia. During the concert in Colorado, the music suddenly fell silent so Phil could engage his fans in what he declared, "Is something very dear to my heart." He went on to share his personal story; that when he was younger he had contracted Hepatitis C and over the years his health had deteriorated to the point he underwent a successful liver transplant. He told the audience, "It's a miracle of modern medicine, and also the result of prayer and healing light that was sent to me by many, many Deadheads, that I am here tonight."

Phil, with the zeal of a Baptist minister, spoke about his new passion—the organ donor program—that had given him a second chance at life. He said, "Organ donation is the key to life for many people. As an organ donor you have the opportunity to save the life of someone you will never meet. So the main thing of what I'm trying to say is, if it is your desire to become an organ donor, it is necessary for you to inform your family because they are the ones who will have to make the decision in a very stressful and grievous, traumatic situation. Just say something like 'In the event of my demise it is my irrevocable desire to be an organ donor.' Your family may still decide not to do it, but at least they will know how you feel about it and what your wishes are."

During the lengthy break in the music, Phil claimed that prior to his operation he had not given much thought to the organ donor program. He said, "I don't know who does think about it, and that's one of the reasons I'm asking each of you in attendance here tonight to become an organ donor; at least think about it now, not just when you need it. Ask yourself this one question—if I am in desperate need of an organ, or if someone I love very, very much is in need of an organ, and that organ is available—would you accept it? The answer, of course, is yes you would. And if the answer is yes, then fair is fair, you should be a donor as well."

That evening, on the way home from the concert, 20-year-old Jon claimed that Phil Lesh had inspired him. He announced to his family that if something bad ever happened to him, he wanted to help others. "I like the idea of saving the life of someone I will never meet." Shortly after that, Jon made it official by changing his driver's license, indicating he wished to become an organ donor.

Music was always an inspiration to Jon. His favorite song, the lullaby his mother sang to him when he was a baby was Bob Marley's *Three Little Birds*. But Jon appreciated an eclectic blend of music, from popular tunes to obscure blues, old-time bluegrass, heavy metal, and even street rap.

Jon had many friends and on the day of his accident he attended a late night party. He drank a few beers and stayed at the party for several hours, leaving abruptly, telling a friend he wanted to sleep in his own bed. Jon-Go was gone.

The accident happened only three miles from the home where Jon was living with his father, Peter, and stepmother, Lois. Whether he fell asleep, or whether alcohol was a contributing factor, was never established. The red Mazda RX-7—the dream sports car Jon had purchased from his grandmother—drifted across the center line, sideswiped an oncoming vehicle and crashed into a tree. At the moment of impact it was estimated the vehicle was traveling at less than 35 miles per hour. The 1987 Mazda was not fitted with a factory airbag, and the impact was so great that Jon suffered immediate brain death. It was 10 long hours before officials could positively indentify the body and notify the next of kin.

Family & Friends

(John Siggins – Jonathan's uncle)

Thinking of Jonathan makes me smile. The two words I would use to best describe Jonathan would be *infectious enthusiasm.* He was a great kid, thoughtful and loving. He made annual visits to our home in Wisconsin and several wonderful memories come to mind. One year he was of that age when boys become gear heads and discover cars and trucks. I had just bought a four-wheel drive diesel pickup and we went out in the back country, making our own roads. Jon was having the time of his life, laughing and enjoying himself.

Another time we were working on the property where our family cabin is located, tearing out an old fence. I put Jonathan to work driving; pulling out fence posts. He had never driven a stick shift, but was willing to learn. The old truck was loaded down pretty heavy and the driver had to be an expert at slipping the clutch. Jonathan had a hard time catching on—probably killed the engine a dozen times—but hand it to the kid, he stayed with it and never gave up. He had some stick-to-it about him, Jonathan did.

We had a Honda Trail 90 and Jonathan wore trails riding it around the property. He was never reckless, but he did like speed. One of my favorite memories is Jonathan and his mom, my sister, Jeanne, on the Honda Trail 90. They are riding and laughing, just having a high ol' time of it.

Even though I only saw Jonathan a couple weeks a year I always felt like we were kindred spirits. When we got the news of the accident—Jeanne called—it was just devastating. She said Jonathan was on life

77

support. I drove her to the airport in Minneapolis, and like most airports they don't allow you to park and wait. But Jeanne was distraught and I wanted to make sure she made her flight. I parked and went inside. I saw a guard approach my car and I went back outside and said I needed a minute. The guard was belligerent and told me in no uncertain terms I needed to move my car. Move it right now! I looked the gentleman in the eye, and in a firm voice informed him my sister had just received news her son was on his deathbed and I was bound and determined to make sure she made her flight so she could be with her son. The man must have been a father because his demeanor changed radically, and with a look of absolute compassion he told me to take my time, that there wasn't a problem.

The next day my family and I caught a flight to California. I thought it important to support Jeanne at such a critical and difficult time, and with four of our five children still living at home, I wanted to provide the opportunity for them to tell their beloved cousin goodbye.

I can't even begin to imagine how traumatic and painful it would be to lose a child. Jeanne handled the situation as well as could be expected. She took great solace in the fact that because of Jonathan's generosity in being an organ donor there was someone out there in dire shape who had received the healthy heart of a 21-year-old. And when that fellow later reached out to Jeanne and called her, it meant the world to her. She told me it was a wonderful feeling to know that Jonathan's heart was beating strong and powering the body of another human being. You can never replace the loss of a child, but Jeanne derived a great deal of comfort and satisfaction in knowing others were benefiting from her tremendous loss.

My hope is that Jonathan's story proves to inspire many others to take stock of what is really important in their lives, and for them to all become organ donors.

(Johnny Siggins – cousin)

Jon was six or seven years older than me, but he was closer to my age than he was to most of the other cousins who were 15 or 20 years older. Jon lived in California and we lived in Wisconsin. We saw each other a couple times a year and he was always my favorite cousin. He was happy and outgoing and took time to include me and our family in the fun.

When Jon came to Wisconsin we usually met at the family cabin on Pike Lake. I remember one time we arrived at the lake and Jon was water skiing and hanging out with some kids his own age, but as soon as he heard we had arrived he dropped what he was doing and came to spend time with us. He was really family oriented. He was someone I looked up to and have tried to emulate.

When the accident happened our family was getting ready to go out for dinner to celebrate my sister's birthday. The phone rang. I answered. Aunt Jeanne asked if Mom or Dad was available. I knew from the panic in her voice that something bad had happened. I handed the phone to Dad. When he finished talking he told us there had been an accident and that Jon was not expected to live. That was so hard to take. That he was gone, just gone like that.

After Aunt Jeanne returned home from California, she told me that Jon had been an organ donor and that the gift of his organs had saved a number of people. I remember thinking how strange it was that Jon's heart was beating inside another human. It seemed that in a way, Jon was still alive. I guess part of him is alive.

When it came time for me to get my driver's license, I checked the box to become an organ donor. I guess I figured that if I could have the kind of impact Jon had, and save the life of even one person, it would be worth it.

(Christine Fera – friend)

Without a doubt, Jeanne is my dearest and oldest friend. We met between our junior and senior years of high school and have remained friends. In so many ways our lives have paralleled each other. We each met what we thought was the love of our life, got married, and each had a single child born within days of each other. The difference was that I had a girl. Over the intervening years life got in the way—we both got divorced and remarried and had our careers—and yet we managed to stay in touch.

I was at work the day I got the call from Jeanne. She was at the airport in Denver, waiting for a connecting flight to San Francisco. She said Johnny had been in a terrible automobile accident and was at Valley Medical Center, the top trauma unit in the Bay Area. I left work early, and as I drove to the hospital I was thinking about what a sweet little boy Johnny was, and how he and my daughter had grown up together. I suppose I was conscious of, and thankful for, the fact it was not my daughter in the hospital. But at the same time I was so dreadfully sorry it was Johnny.

The normal protocol in the ICU is for only one or two visitors to be allowed in the room at a time, and then only during prescribed times. But I guess all bets were off and they lifted the rules and made special concessions for Johnny. When I arrived, Jeanne was there along with Peter and Lois, a priest and several others. Johnny was stretched out across the hospital bed, wearing a pale blue gown, and it was such a terrible shock to see him there because he was so bruised and swollen that he didn't look like Johnny. At that point he was still breathing on his own and I think that gave Jeanne a sense of false hope. But there was no hope, not really. The doctors were trying to stabilize Johnny and were talking about recovering his organs.

The night before the organs were to be taken, a steady stream of visitors came to pay their final respects. The mood in Johnny's room was somber, just so incredibly sad. It made me very mindful of the loss we were all suffering. I know this tragedy made me even more mindful of the importance of the organ donor program. I've been on the donor list for many years, and I'm now also a blood donor; giving blood every eight weeks.

I tried to be understanding and supportive of Jeanne, as she would have done for me if the tables were turned. In the weeks and months after the accident, we spoke often. But I noticed the biggest change in Jeanne's healing process occurred after the heart recipient reached out and contacted her. His name was George and he said he was hours away from death when he received Johnny's heart. He was very appreciative and at the same time very, very sorry for Jeanne's loss. It was a good conversation for Jeanne. She took solace in knowing Johnny's heart was beating in another man's body.

What I take away from all this is the simple fact this could happen at any time to any of us who are mothers or fathers. And if the day ever comes when we have to make such a challenging decision, it is my hope we each decide to do the right thing and allow the doctors to recover the organs of our loved one. If we make that personal sacrifice we will be rewarded with the knowledge we have given the greatest gift of all to others in desperate need.

(Renate Boronowsky – best friend)

Jon and I were born three days apart and it seemed as though we were always connected, like a sister and a brother are connected. Our parents were close friends. I guess when Jon and I were babies we were a funny pair. He would grunt at me and I would cry. Then he would get upset that I was crying and he would cry.

I remember a time when we were maybe eight years old. It was the 4th of July and I was terrified of fireworks. But not Jon. He was the adventure kid. He had no fear, felt no fear. He lit a sparkler and brought it to me, asking me—almost mocking me—if I could handle it. Then he laughed and showed me how to twirl the sparkler and make circles in the dark. He was just such a silly, compassionate, good-hearted kid.

By the time we reached high school, our paths began to veer away from each other, but we kept up on what was going on, mostly through social media. He was snowboarding at Tahoe, hiking in the mountains, surfing. He bought a car, had a girlfriend. After high school I was busy going to cosmetology school and working for a skin care company. In fact, I was working the day I got a call saying Jon had been in a wreck, was in bad shape and they didn't think he was going to make it. I dropped everything and went to the hospital. Walking into the room in ICU was just so surreal. The person I saw on the bed did not look like my friend. Where was that lanky, awkward, goofy, fun-loving, full-of-life kid I remembered?

For a long time I sat beside the bed and wept, and then I picked up the sci-fi book I was reading at the time, *Children of the Mind*, by Orson Scott Card. I began reading to Jon. It was the part of the story where the main character dies, but he doesn't really die, his spirit, his being, is absorbed into everything in the universe.

The words seemed so poignant, so right. I just kept reading.

What makes me the saddest is that I will never get to share all the milestones in Jon's life—college graduation, marriage, the birth of his first child—and he will not be there for mine. If Jon had been alive when I got married, I would have made him wear a dress and be my maid-of-honor. Knowing what a goofball he could be, Jon probably would have done it.

In my estimation the organ donor system is messed up. We should all be donors automatically. If you don't want to be a donor, then you have to make a conscious decision to opt out. The question is, if you die, do you want all your parts in a box? Or do you want to spread those parts around and allow someone to have a grandpa, or a grandma, for a few more months, a few more years? Life can change so fast. In one heartbeat it can change. I'm so glad Jon was an organ donor. It is comforting to know that he goes on, out there somewhere; that his story goes on.

I haven't really told many people this fact—I'm pregnant with twins, a girl and a boy—and our boy is going to be named after my best friend, Jonathan.

(Susan Riley – Jonathan's aunt and godmother)

I am 10 years older than Jeanne. When Mom brought Jeanne home from the hospital I was allowed to skip school. From that day forward it was like Jeanne was my baby. That was the way I viewed our relationship, not so much as sisters, but more as mother/daughter.

When Jeanne was in high school the family moved away to California and we only saw each other when they came home to Wisconsin, usually on vacations to the family cabin at Pike Lake. Those times were filled with much laughter and joy.

I remember when Jon was just a baby, the way he liked to sit on my lap and snuggle. I read him books. He always turned the page and was so excited to see what was on the new pages. As Jon grew, his personality seemed to shine so brightly. He loved his family and friends, had such a full, warm heart and the sweetest smile ever. That smile seemed to stretch from ear to ear. He embraced everyone. He embraced life.

One year we were vacationing at Pike Lake. When we woke up Jon and my youngest son, Patrick, were nowhere to be found. Someone noticed the 4-wheelers were gone and Jeanne and I were worried. Where were those boys? We finally found them in the barn, sitting on the 4-wheelers, listening to music and talking and laughing; boys just being boys.

After graduating from high school it took Jon some time to discover his true passion in life. He found that passion in firefighting. After graduating from college he planned to become a fireman. That is such a demanding profession, and dangerous, but Jon explained it was the best way for him to help others. I think his decision to become an organ donor followed along with that same line of thinking.

Jeanne called me with the news that Jon had been in a terrible accident. She said Jon had been declared brain dead. I told her we didn't know that for a fact, and that we would pray for a miracle. She caught the first flight to California. She had a short layover in Denver and my precious son, Patrick, who lives in Denver, dropped everything and flew to California with Jeanne. I flew out the following day.

All I could do was be with Jeanne, hold her and cry with her. I just wanted to be supportive and to try to comfort her as best I could. It was one of the most difficult times of my life, and when the organ coordinator came and started talking about recovering the organs, that was almost too much for us to endure. Then it seemed to take forever for Jon's body to be stabilized so the organs could be taken. That was the hardest of all, the waiting.

We never gave up hope—miracles do happen—but hope was finally gone as we accompanied Jon's body down the long hallway to the operating room. The organ donor people were waiting there for us. They were standing beside small coolers that looked like coolers for pop and beer. It was shocking to think they would soon be packed with Jon's organs. The reality was sobering. And even though it was weird and strange, it was also an amazing bonding opportunity to share with family. We sang to Jon—*Three Little Birds*—and it was beautiful. It was like we were embracing Jon one last time before sending him off on an incredible journey. Words could never begin to describe the experience: heartbreaking, unbelievable, fantastic, spiritual, humbling, overwhelming, awe-inspiring. I suppose the best way to put it is to say it was a combination of all the emotions a person can feel in a lifetime, rolled into one.

After it was over, for a long time, I had to deal not only with my grief, but also how personally helpless I felt in not being able to take away some of Jeanne's pain. She had to carry that burden alone. In time I came to realize it was enough for me to have been there with her; to cry with her, to hold her in my arms and try to bring her comfort the best I could. That was all I could do.

(Tim Riley – cousin)

Jon was one of the most thoughtful and compassionate people I have ever known. One time we were fishing off the dock at our family cabin at Pike Lake. Jon was probably five years old and I was twice his age. We caught several fish and then Jon suddenly asked me a question, wanting to know if it hurt a fish when it bit the hook. I told him that according to some studies fish were not capable of feeling pain. That wasn't enough for Jon. He wanted to know what I thought. I said I suspected a hook had to cause the fish a certain amount of pain. He said he felt that way too. After that exchange we sat for several minutes and then Jon announced he didn't much feel like fishing any more. I told him I didn't really either. Jon had compassion for all things, including fish.

After Jon's accident—while he was in the hospital on life support—I wanted to do something to honor him, and help him on his transitional journey to his next life. I visited the Buddhist shrine located near Red Feather Lakes, Colorado. Here, in a broad meadow with mountain peaks all around is located the Great Stupa of Dharmakaya, a 108-foot-tall Buddha structure. This is a gathering spot that serves as an inspiration for peace and compassion throughout the world. To me this place, surrounded by the energies of the temple and the surrounding environment, embodied Jon and everything he stood for in his short life.

I sat cross-legged on a devotional pad, meditating, and I don't know how to say it except that I had a shamanic vision, an altered state of mind that was very powerful and helpful to me in reaching an understanding. During this, Jon's presence emerged. I felt him very strongly. It was nothing visual, more a sense that I was now in Jon's company. He was with me, a part of me, and at that moment I had an overwhelming feeling of calmness, and serenity, and contentment. Jon spoke to me without using words; telling me everything was fine, there were no worries, no cares, and he was going to where he needed to go, wanted to go. It was a very spiritually uplifting moment.

That day I took a photograph, and when I looked at it later, above the shrine is a glowing ball of energy, hanging there in the sky. I was never aware of the apparition when I snapped the shot, but it is definitely there in the photograph. You might ask if I think that is Jon's spirit hovering there. Yes, I definitely think so.

(Patrick Riley—cousin)

I am the youngest child in my family with two older siblings. My relationship with Jonathan, since we were only four years apart in age, was more than cousins. I thought of Jonathan as the younger brother I never had. I think he, since he was an only child, thought of me as his older brother. I know, whenever we got together we played and talked like brothers.

When I think of Jonathan, which I do quite often, I always see his smile. It just seemed to radiate fun. He was such a happy soul, and a real joy to be around. Jon was the type of kid who was one hundred percent ready for fun and action. He gave off this vibe of being easy-going and laid-back, but he was always up for any adventure or the next thrill in life. The first time Jonathan and I got to do something outside of family activities was when I came to California. He and I went to Six-Flags Discovery Kingdom in Vallejo. It's a theme park. We rode all the rides and when we came to the bungee jump I asked Jonathan if he was up for it. His reaction was—what are we waiting for? Let's go!

I was living in Colorado, on top of a hill above Boulder. Jonathan came to visit, spotted a long-board and suggested we cruise all the way downtown. We did it, a long, magnificent run, but when we got to the bottom it dawned on us just how far it was back to the house. No worries. Jonathan laughed, stuck out his thumb and we hitched a ride back to the top of our hill. If you spent any time around Jonathan you had to appreciate the good, genuine energy he gave off, it seemed to surround him.

Then came the day when I was out walking my dog, Marley, and my mother called and told me about the accident and that Jonathan was on life support. She said Aunt Jeanne was flying out to California and mentioned she was catching a connecting flight in Denver. Immediately I went to work, researching which flight she was coming in on, and what the connecting flight to San Francisco would be. I booked a seat on that flight, threw together a backpack, and headed for the airport.

It was hard enough for me trying to deal with my own feelings. I couldn't even begin to imagine what Aunt Jeanne was going through. But I wanted to be there for her, to at least make sure she had a shoulder to cry on. When she got to the gate and saw me she was elated—even smiled through her tears—and whispered a thank you, saying it was so sweet for me to meet her. I had to choke back the tears and try and be strong for her. That was difficult.

We boarded the plane, and obviously our seats were not together, but I spoke to a young woman seated next to Aunt Jeanne and explained the situation. She was an angel, very gracious. It was one of those wonderful human moments of absolute compassion. She took my seat and I sat beside Jeanne.

In my mind the flight, landing and getting to the hospital is all a blur of disconnected memories. When we arrived at Jonathan's room there were a number of people there, family and friends, and Aunt Jeanne rushed to her son. She wanted to hold him, to love him, and she broke down like any loving mother would do. Her pain was so incredibly obvious. We all felt so helpless; I know I did.

What struck me about Jonathan was how normal he looked. I don't remember any bruising or swelling. Maybe I blocked that out. He seemed fine, as if he would wake up at any moment, flash a grin and say something like, "Hey, dude, let's get going." That is what I remember.

The process of the organ donation was a long and drawn out affair that took several days. It gave all of us the opportunity to be with Jonathan on our own terms. We put up photographs in the hospital room. Family and friends gathered. We told stories. We laughed. We cried.

My last moments with Jonathan were in the hospital room. I held his hand and Jonathan communicated several things to me. He made me aware that everything was fine, and he indicated to me that he was happy and that I should have no worries. I wanted to know if there was anything I should be doing, could do. Jonathan's response, what I sensed, was that I was already doing it. I was there for his mom. I didn't understand this at the time, but Jonathan specified I was to make sure his story was finished. I asked Jonathan's father, Peter, about that, if Jonathan had been working on a story. Peter was not aware of anything. Then when I heard about this book, *Three Little Birds*, it all became very obvious. Jonathan's story was going to be finished, and he would have the opportunity to touch many lives and get across his message; to be happy, to enjoy life, and for all of us to give like he gave, through the organ donor program.

(Megan Riley – cousin)

I suppose it would be best to allow the reader to know my profession is that of psychic, medium and animal communicator. I have always been intuitive, but for a long time I tried to ignore it, to keep it hidden away. Finally, I came to the realization I needed to own this thing and accept who I am. It may be a little uncomfortable for some to accept, but that is the way it is. My specific reality is that I can see and feel and sense in ways other people cannot, or they refuse to allow themselves to explore these realms.

My introduction to Jon-Jon was when he was maybe six months old and Jeanne and Peter were living in San Francisco. I stepped into the kitchen and Jeanne was there looking absolutely stunning and adorable with an asymmetrical haircut. My eyes were drawn away from her to the baby sitting in a highchair. Little Jon-Jon looked directly into my eyes and I said the first thing that came to me. I said, "You are a child of the light, aren't you?" And in response Jon-Jon burst forth in this lighthearted giggle. I said, "You are here on this earth to teach us." And once again he giggled, blinked his eyes several times and began shoving Cheerios into his mouth. Some people might say such a response is typical of any child, but I read a much different meaning into our interaction. I accepted it as a communication between the two of us, an acknowledgement of sorts, I suppose.

I was 13 years older than Jon-Jon, and as he grew to become a young man what I saw was this wonderful bursting of pure light and energy. He was a loving kid and he was curious; always asking questions. He had this unquenchable thirst to know. Even with complete strangers he would ask very personal questions, and they usually answered. He wanted to know about the things that motivated people, how they came to the decisions they made, and what they wanted to accomplish in their lives. Those are pretty deep concepts for a kid, but Jon-Jon was wise beyond his years.

Although Jon-Jon had this incredibly inquisitive mind, he was a bit of a goofball—physically awkward—but that never bothered him, not for a minute did it bother him. He wore shoes too big, saying they were more comfortable and gave him room to grow. I told him they looked like clown shoes and he just laughed. Sometimes he wore a unicorn mask and other times he might show up with a bucket on his head. He didn't care. He was just Jon-Jon being Jon-Jon.

One time I was having Thanksgiving at my place in Colorado. I live at 9,400 feet above sea level and it can get awfully cold. There was Jon-Jon running around wearing a pair of shorts and flip-flops in the snow. We were going to try frying the turkey, but didn't take into consideration how long it would take the oil to get hot starting out at minus 20 degrees. It was nearly midnight before the turkey was ready to serve. The skin was brown and crispy and the meat moist and deliciously flavorful. I remember the way Jon-Jon thoroughly enjoyed that meal. He was probably starving. As he ate he made all these expressive sounds; sighs, mutterings and groans of pleasure. The other thing I remember about that holiday was that texting was the new thing to do and Jon-Jon was firing off messages to his buddies back in California. When his mother got the bill it was something like five hundred dollars, and she wasn't very happy about that.

Jon-Jon loved food and his favorite meal was always a bacon cheeseburger on a big Kaiser bun with a mountain of french fries—not the Burger King—but the 20 dollar melt-in-your-mouth-hunk-of-bread-and-meat variety. Besides food, Jon-Jon loved his family. I remember him at Pike Lake—he was really into the water and all water-related sports—and he was this big gangly kid and his little cousins were hanging onto his arms and legs as if he was their private monkey gym. And music was big with Jon-Jon. He and I connected on that plane. We both were into music.

It is my belief that those people who are to die young somehow know that fact, that they are not going to be around very long, so they want to experience it all, to take in everything. Jon-Jon was like that. I don't believe he ever imagined himself as old, or even as middle-aged. He knew.

Jon-Jon was my star-seed. Star-seeds are those children of the light who are very intelligent, artistic and grounded. They rarely do well in normal, mundane lives. They are best suited to living on the fringes of life. That was Jon-Jon, a star-seed who might have bloomed during his time on earth, but he will have a much bigger and more important impact from the other side.

After the accident, while Jon-Jon was out of his body, but had not yet been pronounced officially dead, he and I had a metaphysical chat. What he told me, he said it over and over again, was—*It's all good. No worries. It's all good. Just be happy, Dude.*

I wanted to talk to Jeanne, to tell her about my conversation with Jon-Jon and to reassure her, but Jeanne was not in a receptive space. She was still clinging to a sliver of hope that Jon-Jon would return to life, and wrestling with the decision to go along with what Jon-Jon wanted—his final act was to become an organ donor.

About a month after Jon-Jon died, the families from Wisconsin and California all got together in South Dakota to celebrate Thanksgiving. We set a place at the table for Jon-Jon, even poured him a glass of wine. We went around the table and each of us said something about Jon-Jon; what we remembered, or admired, or a funny story. We laughed, and we cried together. It was an extremely emotional time. At one point I looked outside, and perched on a drooping phone line directly in front of the window where we were all gathered, were three little birds. That was Jon-Jon's favorite lullaby, *Three Little Birds*, and I took it as a sign from another dimension that Jon-Jon had joined us.

It happened again—three little birds—when my sister got married. It was a high-vibration event that Jon-Jon, if he had lived, most certainly would have attended. It was held in a beautiful setting in the mountains of Colorado. The family encouraged me to start the ceremony by inviting all those who had departed to come join our celebration. As I was speaking, three little birds appeared and fluttered over the heads of the guests. That choked me up. I stood there laughing and crying at the same time. I knew Jon-Jon, with his goofy, crooked, shit-eating grin, was now part of our celebration.

OBITUARY

Jonathan Ashley Thomas Brown, "Jon", blessed his family and friends for the 21 years since his birth on April 29, 1987 to parents Peter Brown and Jeanne Hancock in Mountain View, California. His passing on October 20, 2008 in San Jose leaves behind Peter, Jeanne, stepmother Lois Brown, stepfather Bill Phillips as well as his grandmother Myrna Brown, grandparents Ray and Peg Siggens, and step grandmothers Sandy Phillips and Francis New. Jon also leaves behind extended family of aunts, uncles and cousins in California, Hawaii, Colorado, Arizona, El Salvador, and Wisconsin, all places Jon loved to visit.

Jon spent his early years living in San Jose, Palo Alto and Mountain View before moving to the Santa Cruz Mountains in 2000. There he met many friends at C.T. English Middle School and continued on with them to Los Gatos High School. These friends would stay with him for the rest of his life.

He was attending Cabrillo College studying computer science. Jon had a real knack for understanding and working on computers. His plans were to first get his BS in engineering and then continue on for a Masters in Philosophy. He had studied philosophy and loved to speak with people about their thoughts and beliefs. He also created extraordinary stories and was able to weave many levels and depth into them. He had recently discovered the power of writing and created some astounding essays.

Jon's favorite activities included snowboarding, surfing, hiking, and spending time with his many good friends. He loved living here in the mountains, and in his own words, said this about the outdoors, "Nature intrigues me, and I can't stop myself from going exploring whenever I get the chance."

Jon also had a heart for animals; growing up with Katie, the family bull terrier, as well as other dogs, cats, and birds. He was wonderful with his young cousins and had incredible patience with children. Jon loved being with people and always gave them time and attention.

His love and genuine thoughtfulness for others made him a joy to be around. He was welcomed into many homes and spent time between his three homes on the mountain, ours and his dear friends, and his homes with Bill and Jeanne in Los Altos and Wisconsin.

It is with gratitude that we look back on the years that we were blessed to spend with him. He will be deeply missed.

Painting of Tootie on a leaf by Donna Hooker

Chapter Six

George slowly became aware of something—consciousness—
drifting with the weightlessness of a falling feather. A vague
suggestion of light touched both eyelids, playing delicately
across the thin membranes, a faint glow moving behind gray
curtains. Eyelids fluttered and reluctantly opened a tiny
fraction, revealing an eerie dullness marbled with tinges of
cream, pink and gold. Individual sensations—one sensation at
a time, sometimes overlapping—came uncertainly at George.
He became responsive to the solidity of his body, cool sheets
touching his skin, the timid obscurity of his surroundings;
blinking green blips of light, pinging sounds and the stark
reality of pain, a crushing perception of pain. Eyelids fluttered,
closed.

Tootie was flying, fighting against a strong headwind. The sky was blue-black with roily clouds below being shredded against serrated mountain peaks. A frosty wetness was falling, not as rain or snow, but as white wads that stung Tootie's eyes. Her eyelids worked; moving up from the bottom to momentarily cover the eyes.

George was with Tootie, flying in unison with her. The only sounds audible were the nasty whine of the wind, the strong, steady beat of Tootie's wings stroking air and the grunting noises she sometimes made with her exertions.

George woke up and became aware of the constricting tube down his throat and the machine breathing for him, pumping air in with a whoosh and sucking air out with an easy rhythm. He remembered a movie he had seen—*Alien*—and had a sense of the same harsh sounds of the way the evil creature breathed. George felt a heavy weight in the middle of his chest. He tried to move, but that weight held him down. He tried to lift a leg. He could do that. He lifted the other leg, flexed his fingers on both hands. Then he lay motionless and tried to understand the where and why of his being.

A woman appeared, and in the glow of the monitors her skin was eerily luminescent. Her face was long and narrow, almost skeletal, and very pretty. Her eyes were her most expressive feature. Any man would fall in love with those eyes. Her hair was blonde and so rich in color and texture that if she pulled it behind her ears and tied it with a rubber band, that hair would still be lovely. The hair fell around her face, framed that divine face like a golden halo. George saw an angel. The angel spoke. "George, can you hear me?" George blinked. The breathing tube was taped to his lips. He could not speak.

"You are doing great," said the angel. Her words were like musical notes. Her smile widened. Her teeth were perfect and very white. "I'm here to take care of you." She seemed to radiate joy and George felt this angel, *his* angel, had been sent specifically to help guide him on his journey. Any tension he was feeling in the moment dissipated like steam. He relaxed under the hypnotically structured tempo of the breathing machine; diaphragm flexing, chest rising, chest falling.

*****

George remembered the Sacramento River in the springtime of his youth. The water was warm and the air carried with it the redolence of the ocean a hundred miles to the west. He could hear the gulls and geese talking and could appreciate the many forms of life held below the surface of the river's waters, as well as along the shores. The golden river flowed through his mind, twisting and turning across the broad Sacramento Valley and he saw the rafts he and his brother had fashioned from driftwood. They played pirates and engaged in mock battles. Never again in his life had George ever felt as content as he had playing with his brother in the summertime on the Sacramento River.

George awoke to a male nurse telling him it was time for the breathing tube to be removed, and to expect a slight amount of discomfort. A hand was placed on George's chest and George wanted to shout, "Don't press on my chest! You will rip me in two!"

"Take a deep breath and hold it. After the tube is removed I want you to cough three times."

George was aware of fingers prying tape away from his cheeks and lips, aware of that hand on his chest, aware of the choking/gagging sensation as the breathing tube was withdrawn from his throat. And then it was over. He had been holding his arms protectively around his chest and now he coughed three times, not big coughs, just small coughs that shot pain through his chest. But he was now breathing on his own.

"That hurt," were the first words he spoke. His voice was thick and raspy. He asked for water and was given a cup of ice chips. They were cold and delicious and took away some of the dryness George felt in his throat.

"Would you like to speak to Donna?" asked the male nurse.

"Sure."

A white phone was handed to George. He stared at it for a long moment, not sure what to do with the instrument and then remembered and held it to his ear. He said, "Hello," into the mouthpiece.

"Hello," said Donna's cheerful voice. "I can't believe I'm actually talking to you."

George thought it was important for him to console Donna and let her know he was awake and doing well. He said, "I'm okay."

Donna seemed pleased with that assessment and went on to say the surgery had gone well, only taking four hours instead of the customary eight. No blood transfusions were needed and that was a good thing, too. She said the doctors reported George was doing, *beautifully*.

"You must be tired," croaked George.

"Haven't slept in 36 hours."

"Get some rest. An angel watches over me."

"I love you."

The phone was taken from George.

*****

When George awoke he was thinking about how much different his life was going to be now that he had a new heart. No longer would exhaustion plague him. No longer would he have to live in fear of suddenly dropping dead. He switched mental gears and wondered about Tootie. After all these many

100

weeks apart would she even recognize him? He thought she would, but still there were nagging doubts.

"My picture," George said to a nurse wearing a white uniform.

The nurse pulled the photograph from where it was tucked beside George. She gave it to him and he studied the photo for a moment and told the nurse, "My Tootie."

"I know," said the nurse.

*****

Donna came into George's hospital room in the ICU and was shocked to find George sitting upright in a chair with a tray on a stand in front of him. He was munching a half slice of dry toast. The first thing she noticed was how George seemed to radiate life. The ashen hue to his skin had been replaced by a pinkish glow. Her hands came to her mouth and she exclaimed, "I can't believe it. I just can't believe it."

George was smiling. He said, "My feet actually feel warm. It's been ages since my feet felt warm. And I can taste again. This toast is fabulous."

Donna had difficulty getting past the many tubes and IVs, but she managed to kiss George and tell him she loved him. He said he loved her too. He asked about Tootie, and Donna assured him that her sister, Carol, who was staying at the house and taking care of Tootie, was keeping Tootie on the same routine and allowing the goose to go outside to feed on grass and fly for exercise.

"Can you call Carol?" asked George. "I'd like to talk to her. Maybe she can hold the phone close to Tootie so she hears my voice and knows I'm okay."

*****

The third day after surgery the rehabilitation nurse came to George's room and told him it was time for him to try and walk. The attempt took a total of five male nurses; two on each side and another to pull along the apparatus holding the monitors and IV bags. George was like an infant just learning to walk. He told his legs to move, but they did not respond on command. His legs had to be maneuvered manually until he got the hang of it. Each step was an ordeal.

Over the next few days, tubes and IVs were gradually removed. George got stronger and when he became mobile, he was transferred from the ICU to the 11 K ward. He had been at 11 K before surgery, when he was experiencing heart failure and waiting for a donor heart to be located. It was like a homecoming as the nurses came around to welcome him back to the ward like an explorer returning from distant ports is hailed as a hero in his homeland.

Each doctor who visited George's room was met with the same question from George, "Can I go home?" He was tired of looking out the windows at the foul Willamette Valley winter weather, the sky riding low, heavy and as gray as wet cement. Rain and more rain was all there ever was to see, but once in a great while the clouds parted and in the far distances George saw triangular mountain peaks—Hood, Adams, St. Helens—gleaming under a coat of pearly white snow. Those moments were dramatic for George because he knew that over that far-flung chain of mountains—the Cascade Range—was his part of Oregon, the dry side. If he crossed over those mountains and traveled several hundred miles south he would be home. He wondered how long it would take Tootie to fly that distance and figured if she flew at 20 miles per hour, which he thought she was capable of flying, it would take one long day. Just one long day and he and Tootie could be reunited.

When George was not walking the long hospital hallways for exercise, he usually sat in front of the big window in his room. One day he observed a gray squirrel dodging across the lawn below, scampering up a tree and climbing to a limb very near his window. The bushy tail flowed like water over the bare-boned limb; legs dangling, head held low. A passing breeze stirred the air, lifting the squirrel's eyelashes and the squirrel twitched its nose as if appreciating the breeze. Then it got up, and without seeming to expend any effort, jumped from limb to limb, gamboling its way higher and higher until slender branches swayed under its weight. The dark shadow of a hawk came sailing overhead and the squirrel switched positions, hanging from the underside of a thin branch so as not to be exposed and run the risk of suffering death by talons.

When Donna came to visit, George told her every last detail of his encounter with the squirrel. It was, without a doubt, the most exciting and dramatic experience of George's otherwise dull day. That realization distressed him and made him all the more anxious and homesick.

George regained his strength and the pain in his chest subsided. With Christmas drawing near, and having all the medical apparatuses that had encumbered and limited him now removed, the doctors informed George he could leave the hospital. But for the next two months, with constant appointments and scheduled heart biopsies—the insertion of a slender claw-like device into a vein to recover a small amount of tissue from the heart, and having that tissue checked for the possibility of his body rejecting the new heart—he was required to stay in Portland. George and Donna moved into the home of a friend near the Willamette River. The change in scenery, and his newfound liberation, helped to buoy George's spirits. He was almost giddy.

Now the days were spent walking. George and Donna, hand-in-hand, walked city sidewalks glistening with rain, stepping around puddles and pools of water where raindrops boomeranged; sometimes just standing and watching steady rain shimmer under street lamps like dancing strips of silver foil. They listened to the slick sucking noises of tires on wet asphalt and when they reached the traffic light at the bottom of the hill, they paused to view the daily progress of a crew building yet another Walgreens store—bricklayers on scaffolds, coolers with drinks and their lunches beside them—and heavy equipment moving around in what would soon become a parking lot. Crossing the street at the light, they passed a McDonald's where deep fat fryers pumped greasy smells that swirled and seeped into the damp air. A long block away was a business complex with a Big Star and a Meier and Frank. If the weather was especially bad, George and Donna walked the floors of the spacious mall and looked at the dizzying array of gifts waiting for some shopper with a credit card to buy them and take them to a transitory home under a Christmas tree.

The sky became even a deeper shade of gray and the air grew colder. Evening descended and the lights took on the sickly orange haze of civilization. It began to snow sparse, dry flakes. Now George and Donna walked with hands stuffed in coat pockets and their breaths bloomed before them like white flowers. Before they got back to their friend's house, the snow was intensifying with flakes so fine they looked as though they had been sifted before falling to earth. Snow floated around street lights and was swirled by passing traffic. Night sounds were muffled; a horn honking, the gunning of a car engine, the whine of spinning tires and from an apartment building a door slammed and a man called a woman's name—Mary or Sherry. They passed a neighborhood bar emitting a mixture of pleasant and unpleasant perfumes and odors, and where strong drinks were dispensed along with the raucous monotone of a radio rapper that seeped through other noises like blood in water.

To warm up they stopped at a Starbucks and had hot chocolate, stirring the drinks with swizzle sticks and wrapping their fingers around the cardboard cups to steal the warmth. They sipped and talked about home and how quiet and nice it would be to sit in their living room and watch the snow come down. They talked about Tootie. The one subject they avoided, never mentioning it on purpose, was the fact the new heart beating steadily in George's chest had to have come from someone. A person had died so George could live.

That night a big storm blew in. Wind rattled the windows like teeth chattering in a cold face and bare limbs shook and scraped against the siding. By morning, a foot of snow had fallen, bringing the citizens of Portland to their collective knees. The streets were deserted. George and Donna, used to living in snow in their home near Bonanza, pulled on their boots and walked through the quiet wonderland. The haze of pollution hung thick and a weak sun tried to struggle through the mass of clouds the color of an ancient scar. The unplowed streets were as confusing as a ball of twine and on one corner George stood with legs planted firmly apart, arms hanging loose, enjoying the sparkle of the snow, the glitter of neon and the stonework of grand buildings. He broke the quiet to say, "I can't wait to get home."

*****

Shortly after the arrival of a new year, George and Donna were given the news they had been waiting to hear—George was being released and he could return home. The doctors and nurses presented George with a huge get-well card signed by all of them, and a bag of birdseed for Tootie. For the next year George would have to make monthly visits to OHSU for heart biopsies, but that seemed like a small price to pay for the privilege of being allowed his freedom.

*****

Even though OHSU had officially released George, he still had to wait overnight for the results of the latest biopsies. He spent the evening and the following morning loading their pickup truck with their belongings. Under strict orders from Donna, George tried to not overdo. His movements were slow and steady. Finally, that afternoon the phone rang and the transplant coordinator said the test results were perfect, and yes, he was free to leave Portland.

George and Donna left before dawn, driving to the nearest freeway on-ramp and headed due south. By midmorning they had reached Willamette Pass. The only ice on the highway was in shaded spots, otherwise it was clear sailing. As they crested the summit of the Cascades, George looked over the flat, white sheen of ice that covered Odell Lake and the exposed mountain peaks beyond and said, "This makes me happy. I feel like I can finally breathe again."

The one dark cloud on the horizon was George's gnawing fear that Tootie, during their long separation, had forgotten him. As they traveled the busy highway skirting Klamath Lake the familiar pyramid-shaped landmark of Mount McLoughlin came into view. Chuck Berry was on the oldies radio station singing *My Ding-a-Ling*, and in spite of any misgivings George might have had about his reunion with Tootie, he kept beat to the tune, tapping a forefinger on the steering wheel while he and Donna laughed and sang the ridiculous lyrics.

*****

George slipped inside the house and sat on the sofa. The long drive had been exhausting and he was tired, but he was also very anxious, especially with Tootie as close as the next room. He heard Donna open the door to the back porch and all the sounds Tootie made in greeting. When Tootie waddled into the living room and saw George she came to an abrupt stop. She stood in one spot, elongated her neck as high as possible and turned her head from side to side. She was having a difficult time recognizing George. He had gained 35 pounds, had a beard and his skin was now pink and healthy looking.

"How's Daddy's little girl?"

With those words spoken, it was as if a switch was thrown. Tootie honked wildly and rushed to George. He slid off the sofa and onto his knees. Tootie lavished him with goose kisses, beat her wings triumphantly and wrapped those wings protectively around George as if to embrace him. She squawked and made gurgling sounds and began to busily preen George's hair, beard and even his eyebrows. George was bawling. Donna was bawling. And when Carol came into the room, she bawled too.

George and son, Brian, posing with the 1937 Chevrolet, circa 1985

Chapter Seven

Winter lost its icy grip and spring was pushing up crocuses. The snow was melting and bare patches of ground were turning green. Tootie ran her beak through the emerging grasses as she made noises low in her long throat. She fussed with her appearance and took oil from the gland located near her tail, and dabbed it on her feathers. Her communicating was not only the sounds she made but also head motions and body language. If she perceived a threat she looked to George, and if he moved quickly she reacted by extending her wings and searching for that danger. If a hawk or eagle was passing overhead Tootie ducked low, hugged the ground, opened her beak wide, hissed and ruffled her feathers.

"Daddy look for *bities*."

In the language George and Tootie shared, *bities* were hawks, eagles and owls. If no *bities* were within sight, Tootie was free to fly. She flew up to the roof or circled the house. She never flew any farther than that. She purposely stayed close to George.

In the shop, George was putting the finishing touches on the '37. The frame had been modified, the rear end narrowed, a Camaro front end dropped into place and the body and fenders had been worked over and were primed and ready for paint. George had built up a big block Chevy engine and it was ready to mount. The car was nearing completion.

*****

For eight wonderful months, George worked on his car and played with Tootie. He had the strength, stamina and confidence to be able to do exactly what he wanted to do. And then one morning he woke up experiencing an unusual itching sensation on his scalp and face. It felt as if his skin was moving, crawling. He supposed it was some sort of reaction to the medication he was taking, the anti-rejection medication. Next time he visited the doctors—he was still making monthly trips to OHSU in Portland for heart biopsies—he would mention it. He figured this was nothing more than a temporary condition, something that could easily be fixed with a change in medication. He told himself it was no big deal.

George was in the garage when he became nauseous. He stepped outside and vomited. His skin felt damp with perspiration, and clammy, and he sensed he was running a fever. He was probably coming down with something, most likely the flu. He told himself to just tough it out. But the symptoms escalated. He had the shakes, became dizzy and was unable to focus. He could not even hold a wrench on a nut. Finally he stopped trying to work, went to the house and announced he was sick.

Donna promptly put George to bed. She took his temperature and the thermometer inched from 101 to 102, and when it topped out at 103 she placed a call to OHSU. The doctor on duty advised Donna to call an ambulance and have George immediately transported to the nearest hospital. She dialed 911 and asked assistance from the Bonanza EMTs. The volunteer crew arrived and loaded George in the ambulance. They started for Klamath Falls and Sky Lakes Hospital. Donna jumped in the pickup truck and followed.

Crossing Yonna Valley the ambulance engine coughed, lost power and quit running. The driver eased off the highway and parked on a recently harvested alfalfa field. Donna was in a panic. She wanted the EMTs to load George in the back of the pickup and she would drive him to the hospital. But she was informed AirLife had been alerted and a helicopter had already been dispatched. Within minutes a blue and white helicopter was hovering overhead, the wash from the spinning rotors made the stubby alfalfa shimmy and shake. The helicopter set down in the field and the EMTs loaded George inside. By this time George's body was in the grip of a seizure. He was convulsing, suffering hallucinations and mumbling incoherently. Donna refused to leave her husband. She abandoned the pickup in the field and climbed in the helicopter.

The doctors at OHSU were apprised of George's deteriorating condition and made the decision to bypass Sky Lakes Hospital and have George transferred by jet from Klamath Falls to Portland. At PDX an ambulance was waiting and George was whisked down the freeway at rush hour with lights flashing and siren blaring under a Code 3. He was admitted to OHSU hospital and doctors worked to stabilize him as a battery of tests were conducted to try and determine the cause of his sickness.

The only information the doctors were able to share with Donna was that it appeared from an MRI that George was suffering with brain lesions. They could not speculate why he had developed them, but the imagery clearly showed five lesions attached to the left side of George's brain. The left side of the brain is responsible for motor skills, memory and personality. The doctors referred to this as a *life-threatening* situation. Donna wanted to know if the brain lesions and George's new heart were somehow related. The doctors did not know.

*****

All that George can recall of this critical event was the spinning blades of the helicopter as he was being transferred from the broken down ambulance. He does not remember the flight to Portland or the Code 3 ambulance ride at the height of rush hour. When he woke up, his world was as jumbled as a puzzle dumped from a box and strewn across a tabletop. He recognized he was lying on a hospital bed—his body was—but his distorted perception had retreated to the ceiling and was crammed into a far corner. George calmly watched uniformed nurses and doctors dressed in scrubs call out numbers; blood pressure was too low, heart rate too high and erratic. Three times shock paddles were activated. Three times the body on the bed jumped and convulsed.

What occurred to George's twisted out-of-body mind was that the medical staff was there not to save him, but to bring him harm. His irrational thinking screamed at him, telling him, "Quit being a pussy. Fight back!"

The body on the bed—George's body—began to struggle. He fought like a wild animal, ripping loose the heart monitor attached to his chest and throwing it across the room. He swung with his fists and kicked his legs. He bit and scratched and clawed.

Male nurses overpowered George and a groan began from deep in his chest, escaped and came up his throat and out of his mouth as a frightful screech. His arms and legs were strapped to the bedrails. When resisting was no longer an option, the body stopped fighting. Blood was drawn. A strong sedative was administered. George flew from the far corner and reluctantly returned to the body on the bed. After that he remembered nothing.

*****

In his state of unconsciousness George had dreams. In one he was transported to a foreign land. He stumbled up a narrow ravine. Dry leaves crackled beneath his feet and the predominant smell was the biting tang of silver sagebrush. He saw shiny chunks of obsidian lying here and there, as if some ancient tribesman had been here fashioning arrowheads. He could taste the crispness of the air on his tongue. This desolate place seemed both recognizable and yet otherworldly.

George continued to climb. He was very tired, and yet he forced himself to continue, deliberately placing one foot in front of the other, climbing higher, ever higher. The ravine was steep and deep and only a narrow strip of blue sky was visible directly overhead. George did not know what he might find at the top of the ravine, when he crested the summit, but that was his driving force. He was fearful of what he might find, and yet he had a burning desire to know. That quest propelled him.

George came to a sandy spot, an unusually flat area on the face of the vertical terrain. It was so inviting, this level place was, that George thought maybe he should lie down and rest; rest for just a few minutes. Yet he knew, if he chose to rest, he would never rise. He would die there, and when his body was found people would say he had given up; that he had allowed himself to die. George could not accept such a judgmental summation—that anyone might think he was a quitter—so he kept moving forward, one step at a time, moving forward, climbing, climbing.

*****

Donna came into George's room. The restraints binding George had been removed. He was sitting with the back of the bed tilted up. The last time Donna saw George was when he was being transferred from the ambulance and was being admitted to the hospital. She had not been allowed to see him during the crisis. Now, at first glance, her husband seemed perfectly normal. Donna began to smile as she crossed the room to give George a kiss. But as she drew near, George threw up his hands and became highly agitated. He shouted for a nurse.

"She has a knife! She's gonna stab me!"

Donna came to an abrupt stop. The nurse on duty stepped between George and Donna and motioned Donna toward the door. Even after she had exited the room, George continued shouting, "Get her out of here! That woman is trying to kill me!"

The nurse followed Donna into the hallway where she explained, "George is in an altered mental state. He strikes out at everyone. Don't take it personally."

But how could Donna not take such a thing personally?

*****

The lead doctor spoke to Donna about the brain lesions that George had developed. He explained it was now necessary to obtain a biopsy from one of the lesions. The biopsy would reveal information about a possible cause, and the specific type of lesion they were dealing with. An MRI had already pinpointed the locations, and the doctor explained the biopsy would be taken from the lesion directly above George's left eye. A small hole would be drilled in the skull and a slender tube with a claw-like feature—the same type of instrument used for heart biopsies—would be inserted and a small sample obtained. A team of doctors would evaluate the results and make an assessment to determine the best possible course of action. Donna was asked to give her consent to the operation. She dutifully signed her name to the bottom of the form.

When Donna stepped into George's room, she found him heavily sedated. Some of the hair at the top of his forehead had been shaved, and near the hairline, above the left eye, lines had been drawn with what appeared to be a felt marker. There was a small dot that, to Donna, represented where surgeons planned to drill the hole. Even though she had been advised this was the proper course of action, she felt a cramp of panic, experiencing physical anguish; a shiver that gripped hard at her diaphragm and kept her from breathing. The feeling passed. She breathed again. Resolutely she knew she had to go along with what the doctors were recommending. What else could she do?

*****

George was a caveman. He lived in a cave and wore furs from the animals he had killed. He hunted mastodons and woolly mammoths, giant sloths and saber-toothed cats. His world was a very dangerous place. Now he sat in front of a fire at the entrance to his cave, chewing meat off a bone and making guttural sounds. Language had not yet been developed.

Donna eased into George's room and found him—head bandaged—sitting naked on his bed. He was scowling and going through the motions of gnawing on something imaginary he was holding with both hands. He emitted scary noises, like a savage beast will do; snarling, growling, grunting and belching. The nurse in the room, as if this was an every day occurrence, stated, "He thinks he's a Neanderthal."

"A caveman; he thinks he's a caveman?"

Donna had never heard of such a thing—a grown man suddenly becoming a caveman. She left the room and marched to the doctor's office and demanded an explanation. The doctor patiently explained that medicine is not an exact science, and that sometimes patients react in bizarre ways. He suggested to Donna that she not overreact.

"Overreact? My husband thinks he's a goddamned caveman and you think I'm overreacting."

It was explained that George's behavior was more than likely just a phase he was going through, a role he was acting out, a temporary condition. His current state of mind could be caused by his reactions to medications, or by the *root cause* of the brain lesions, whatever that might be. The *root cause* had not yet been determined, but after the results of the biopsy, the consensus among the team of doctors was pointing to a form of *cryptococcus gattii*, a fungus that typically lives in the environment in many tropical and sub-tropical areas of the world. People breathe in the microscopic fungus and it can affect the lungs, central nervous system, or cause brain lesions.

Donna repeated the word "tropical"—they had not visited any tropical climates—and the doctor went on to say that global warming may have allowed for the emergence of the fungi into parts of the world where it had previously never been seen. In recent years, 227 cases had been reported in British Columbia, Washington State and Oregon. Nineteen patients had died from complications of the disease.

"We don't know for a fact he has cryptococcus," said the doctor. "But his cyclosporine count was dangerously elevated—three times what is considered a normal level. We are conducting further tests. He could have contacted the spores when you were walking around Portland after the heart transplant operation. It appears most patients who have become infected are HIV positive, or have compromised immune systems. Because George is taking anti-rejection medication, he might be more susceptible to such a disease."

"How long has he had it?"

"Incubation times vary; anywhere from two to eleven months after exposure."

"Can it be treated?"

"Some forms, yes. With your husband, we have begun an aggressive antibiotic program."

"Will he be okay?"

"We hope so," said the doctor, but his tone was far from comforting or reassuring or convincing.

*****

A nurse stopped Donna outside George's hospital room. "Just so you know," the nurse warned, nodding toward the closed door, "Today he thinks he's an Appalachian moonshiner."

George was sitting in the chair beside the bed. Again he was naked. When Donna entered the room he seemed to recognize her. He smiled, and in a nasally voice she had never heard before—a voice as cold and hard as tombstone granite, and laced with a liberal dose of hillbilly twang—George asked, "Well, sweet-cheeks ya'all come ta get yur white lightnin'?"

Even though Donna had been forewarned, she was still not prepared for this and stood near the door, not daring to come any nearer to her husband.

117

George rubbed a hand over the grizzled stubble on his chin and said, "You ain't no revenuer now is ya, dawlin'?"

"I'm your wife."

"Okay, if ya ain't no revenuer we can do some bidness," stated that irritating voice. "Twenty bucks a quart. How many jars ya want?"

Donna shook her head. She reasoned there was no use trying to communicate with George when he was in such an altered state as this. She turned away, opened the door and was starting to leave the room.

George responded by waving an arm as if to dismiss Donna. "All them there vultures, they up there in da sky just awaitin' ta clean up the countryside. They circle an' circle on them big ol' wings. All they be doin' is looking fir some work." George laughed like a lunatic.

After Donna was gone, George sat and watched the night come on. The bare bones of tree branches faded, and the lights of the city winked on and burned like lively coals. It seemed as if that far away world he was viewing was turning on some separate axis. George sat unmoving, staring at the hot belt of lights that ran the chord of the dark vault before him. He placed his hands on the arms of the chair and pressed against them in the dire hope the the dead center of his universe would dissolve the life beyond the window glass—all of the taut and trembling that he felt alive under his hands—would prove something. He did not know what he wanted it to prove, but something. He said aloud in the dark, "When ya'all be comin' fir y'ur shine?"

Later that night he was walking through a deep forest of deciduous trees, down a long, dark corridor, stepping through pockets of moonlight, pockets of shadow, where the air smelled of rosin and wet stone and no birds sang. He was on the way to his still, back up on the slope where a freshwater spring bubbled forth from the black earth.

*****

George was no longer a moonshiner. He had reverted back in time and now thought he was a baby. He sucked his thumb and was wearing adult diapers—his request—and nothing more than those diapers. He sensed a memory, a vague recollection from long ago when the family lived in the farmhouse along the Sacramento River. George was in bed. His mother came into the room and stood by the window. She talked about the wind and the rain that had come that day and how much she enjoyed the smell of the soil after a good rain like that. She reminisced about when she was young, back during World War II when she served in the USO and sang and danced for the troops, helping put on shows to take the fighting men's minds off the war. She seldom mentioned those years, but when she did it was always with a sense of nostalgia; as if she longed for that part of her life, a part that had been all too fleeting and would never return. She lovingly tucked the blanket around George's shoulders and leaned down to kiss his cheek. He feigned sleep. He smelled her perfume—the scent lush, sweet, floral—and out of one partially open eye George caught a quick glimpse, a silhouette of her breasts, and felt embarrassed. He laid there unmoving, just listening, and heard his mother walk down the hall to her bedroom; heard the bed springs creak and groan when she got into bed, and then there was silence.

"Baby want food."

"The tray is right in front of you," said the male nurse who had come into the room and was tending George. "Feed yourself."

"Feed baby."

The nurse was used to this character. George had been a baby for several days and the nurse, knowing George was on the verge of throwing a tantrum if he did not get his way, picked up the spoon and fed George bites of food off the gray plate on the pink tray. George took a bite and swallowed. Sometimes, if it was a vegetable he did not care for, he refused to open his mouth. Other times he spit out his food and the nurse had to clean up the mess.

To help contain the messes, a large baby bib with cute stick figures and real buttons was tied around George's neck at meal time. He loved that bib, traced his fingers over the stick figures, played with the buttons, and made tut-tut sounds. If George ate everything on his plate, the male nurse rewarded him and allowed George to play with his set of keys. George rattled the keys and was absolutely enthralled at the clinking sound and the way light sparkled off the silver and gold colors.

George liked it when that woman came to visit him. He seemed to recognize her but was not sure who she was. He did not have an understanding of why she came to visit him so often. Her voice had a lovely, reassuring quality—as comforting as the sound of a stream of rushing water—that was vaguely familiar to George. He liked to look into her expressive blue eyes and when she came she sat near and showed him photographs. She told him this picture was taken on the day they were married, and this was the '37 Chevy he was restoring, and this was his pet goose, Tootie. Each time Donna showed a photograph of Tootie, George became animated, waving his arms and kicking his legs and excitedly repeating, "Goose! Goose! Goose!"

"Do you know who I am?" asked Donna, removing the photograph and leaning close so George could see her.

George stared at her for a long moment. His brow was knit in deep concentration. At long last he said, "Donna."

*****

George was imagining a wilderness camp. There was a narrow band of evening sky; the golden light fading to red as evening deepened to the darker shades of dusk. A band of wild horses was coming in off the desert to a waterhole. The surface of the water was polished blue-black. The horses came in snorting and stamping their front feet; skittery in their approach, as if unable to find the proper gait. The day's heat was dissipating up from the sandy soil and the air above was turning cool under the open canopy of emerging stars. A chestnut mare, with four white stockings and a blaze down her nose stepped forward and leaned her head down; muzzle breaking the flat plane of the water, quivering lips sending little waves rippling across the pond. Other horses moved forward. The lead stallion, a light colored roan, was the last to drink.

Later, a bank of clouds moved in, obscuring the stars, and rain came slanting down. The mustangs moved from out of the darkness and stood at the edge of the firelight. Their hair was slick and their red eyes burned like hot embers in the night.

*****

Thoughts and memories came to George like he was chasing sliced peaches with a spoon around a glass dish. They were too slippery for him to actually ever get hold of. Anything in his brain was fair game. All his ghosts were on the loose.

*****

"George has learned to walk. He is ambulatory. His condition has been stabilized," the doctor explained to Donna. "We feel as though, here at OHSU, that we have done all we can do."

121

"He's no longer a caveman, or a moonshiner, or a baby," said Donna, "but he's hardly stable. Is he ever again going to be my George, the man I married?"

"We don't have the ability to definitively answer that question," the doctor bluntly stated. He glanced at his watch, wanting at that moment to be somewhere, anywhere but talking to the wife of a patient whose behavior could not be explained in clinical terms and quantitative absolutes.

The doctor said, "We feel, at this time, that it would be in the patient's best interest to transfer him to a transitional care facility. I took the liberty of arranging to have your husband admitted to the Plum Ridge facility in Klamath Falls. He will be close to your home, and you can visit him on a regular basis. In the estimation of his team of doctors, this is the best case scenario for all involved."

*****

George was discharged from OHSU on a day filled with dark, moody clouds. Medicare refused to pay for transporting George so it fell to Donna to drive him the 300 miles to Klamath Falls. She was not sure she could control George by herself and took a friend, Linda Hartenberger, along on the trip. In an attempt to head off any trouble, they put George between them in the pickup truck as they headed south on I-5. Even though they had taken this precaution, George kept trying to reach past Linda and open the door. He said, "I wanna get some air moving in this joint." Linda rolled down the window. When George reached for the steering wheel, Donna pushed his hand away along with a strong admonishment, "Don't do that."

They stopped for gas in Oakridge and George got out and stood beside the pickup. He said he wanted to ride in back where he would have more room. He insisted on riding in back. Donna repeated, "No. No. No."

"Where did you get this piece of shit?" George demanded to know, making a sweeping gesture the length of their pickup truck. "Why the hell did you buy this piece of shit?"

"I didn't buy this piece of shit. You did," countered Donna. "Now get in and be quiet."

*****

When George was young he liked to read and maybe he had come across the name Plum Ridge in a Western. *Plum Ridge was a wide-open town visited by drifting cowboys fresh off cattle drives and long overdue for some fun. They drank in the saloons, danced with the pretty girls, fought in the street and more than a few died here. If memory serves correctly, the vigilantes hung three men from the steel railroad bridge that crossed the river below town. Not long after the railroad had been built, a conductor roused a drunken cowboy to inquire as to his destination. The cowboy grumbled, "I'm headed straight ta hell." The conductor promptly stopped the train, had the engineer reverse the engine, and put the cowboy off at Plum Ridge.*

*****

George stepped slowly, cautiously into the commons area at the Plum Ridge facility. He looked around the open room at people sitting slumped in wheelchairs, heads bowed. He had a foreboding sense about the place and the people there. It was as if a strange malevolent spirit had brushed against him on its way out and he stood breathing in unpleasant smells and listening to the sounds of labored gasping. From somewhere a whisper on the edge of hearing could be distinguished. The words were indistinguishable, and yet they disturbed George. Was someone talking about him? He did not know. He tried to draw a breath, but it was as if the others had already stolen all the oxygen in the room.

George made his way from the disquieting commons area and down a long hallway. He was confused about which door to open and wandered aimlessly until a staff member happened along and directed George to his room. He walked in and sat in a chair surrounded by awkward silence. The only illumination in the room leaked from a light on the wall with an opaque plastic shade. George's eyes fixed on nothing; not on the sparse furnishings—beige walls, desk, swivel chair, bed, or a landscape watercolor depicting trees, lake and mountains in stark washes that bled one into another. The predominant smell in the room was of disinfectant that hid other more revolting smells. George felt a rush of aloneness and that surprised him. He did not think he had ever felt alone like that, never before in his life. He sensed more than heard a soft tapping at his door, like three strokes with a sable brush, and then a woman—was it his mother?—was there to comfort him. A hand was rubbing George's neck and massaging the long thin, taut bands of muscles on either side of his spine. George heard a voice asking him what the trouble was.

"I don't know. Things ain't right. I can't remember. I don't know who I am."

*****

Nearly every day Donna made the 40-minute drive to visit George. His mental condition—wound as tight as a cuckoo clock—tottered on the shaky brink between a slim ability to reason and rationalize, and absolute lunacy. Even more frustrating to Donna was that, as time went on, George gave no outward signs of improvement, or even the possibility of improvement. It seemed as though George was taking uncertain steps down an endless stairway to nowhere. He had misplaced, or lost entirely, his personality, behavior and individuality. In their place, George had assumed the traits of those around him. Sometimes he sat in one position, unmoving, for hours. He stared off into space. He mumbled to himself. He drooled. It seemed that any hope for a future, his future, was nothing more than a steady decline into a vegetative state of unresponsiveness.

One time when Donna came to visit, George was sitting on the floor with his legs spread wide. A child was rolling a ball to him. George clumsily caught the ball and rolled it back to the child. Another time Donna found George sitting in a wheelchair with his head hanging low, repeatedly making tiny noises like footfalls creaking on snow. He had become an unattractive facsimile of all those who had been crushed by old age, crushed by life, crushed by disease. The medical system was failing George. Donna could take no more of this. She refused to have her husband warehoused for the remainder of his life. She cried out, "Damn-it all! I'm mad as hell!"

Because George was incapable of representing himself, Donna intervened on his behalf. She bucked the system. The supervisor on duty tried to head Donna off, but Donna stood firm. She checked George out of the facility and took him home.

When George walked into their living room he stopped and looked around like he might have remembered some things, or at least remembered being there at a time in his past. His jaw was slack and he was unsure of what he was supposed to do or how he was supposed to act and react. Donna led him to the sofa. He took a seat. Now he looked agitated and nervous. His body shook, legs bounced up and down and his hands were balled into hard fists.

Donna stepped onto the porch and opened the door for Tootie. The goose walked inside—never made a sound—and went directly to George. She hopped onto the sofa, leaned the weight of her body against George and placed her long neck across his chest. George immediately stopped shaking. His legs stopped bouncing. His fingers loosened their tight grip.

*****

Donna and George fell into a routine. Each morning she fixed breakfast, and while she was washing the dishes she sent George outside to exercise Tootie. Being with Tootie always calmed George. All his tensions and the inner-turmoil he seemed to be experiencing simply dissipated when he was with his goose.

Donna constantly challenged George to remember. She showed him photographs and told him stories. "Remember, after the coyote killed the mother goose, I brought the only egg I could find home. And you hatched it. Yes you did. You put that egg in the bed with you. The next day it hatched. Do you remember that, George?"

George nodded like he actually was remembering, and maybe he was. He had a far away look in his eyes. Judging by his expression, whatever memory he was imagining was a pleasant one.

Most days, after George had eaten lunch and taken a short nap, Donna took him to the shop. She made sure the Sirius XM radio was tuned to the '50s—thinking the music from George's growing up years would be good medicine. She patiently showed George his various tools. She handed him a socket driver and told him what it was and how it was used; handed him a screwdriver and explained it could set a screw or loosen a screw; handed him a piece of sandpaper and showed him how, wrapped around a block of wood, it could take a layer of rust off metal. She was very methodical, concise and always displayed infinite patience with George.

*****

Music blared from the Sirius XM radio.

Maybellene, why can't you be true
Oh Maybellene, why can't you be true
You've started back doing the things you used to do

As I was motivatin' over the hill
I saw Maybellene in a Coup de Ville
A Cadillac a-rollin' on the open road
Nothin' will outrun my V8 Ford
The Cadillac doin' 'bout ninety-five
She's bumper to bumber rollin' side by side

Maybellene, why can't you be true
Oh Maybellene, why can't you be true
You've started back doing the things you used to do

*****

Donna showed George the car he had been working to restore. Pieces and parts of the '37 Chevy were scattered around the room. The big block engine sat on a stand that could be rolled around from place to place. "This is your car," coaxed Donna. "You were fixing up this hot rod before you got sick. Do you remember?"

George shook his head. He did not remember. He thought maybe he could recognize some things; the engine he had rebuilt himself, the fenders that he had straightened and sanded and primed and now were hanging from the ceiling waiting for paint. Those objects were slightly familiar. His memory was beginning to work.

"I'm going to paint it red," mumbled George.

"Yes you are. You remember don't you?"

*****

During the 1960s when back-to-the-land was getting kick-started into a movement, convincing real estate developers were busy subdividing the area north of Bonanza into small acreages and promoting it to Southern California buyers as an Oregon Shangri-La. Sales teams armed themselves with fancy brochures depicting a pristine lake surrounded by tall cottonwoods and luxurious pine trees. In reality, the lake was a shallow holding pond that filled with runoff in the spring and quickly evaporated into a long, sandy flat of short, dry grasses. A drove of Golden State refugees bought into the illusion of Klamath Forest Estate, and with a thousand dollars down and easy monthly payments, they quit their jobs and moved north on a hope and a promise. Others were more practical and patiently waited to retire before they moved north and onto their property.

The subdivision where George and Donna lived was inhabited by these back-to-the-land neighbors. For the most part they were conservative in their thinking, stayed to themselves and were content to live a quiet existence. The home that George and Donna lived in was set on a slump-shouldered ridge above the surrounding neighbors. As the sun set behind the ridge the assembled clouds turned into all the colors of the rainbow; vibrant shades of red, yellow and gold, bleeding off into delicate shades of pink, purple, violet and lavender. Off to the east, across the dry lakebed, the ravines and hollows took on colors as did the tall cottonwoods surrounding the dry lake. Those times Donna and George climbed the ridge, which they did quite often, they looked across broad Yonna Valley. Sprinklers rhythmically squirted water from pivots and hand lines on the green of the valley floor. Off to the north was a low pass where a blacktop road twisted and turned on the way to Sprague River. The western horizon was dominated by the gray hump of the long hill behind Dairy, an unincorporated community featuring a few houses, one roadside restaurant and a feed store with a scale out front for the convenience of farmers, ranchers and truck drivers; so they could weigh cattle, hay, wheat, potatoes and other crops.

"Do you know the name of the man who runs the feed store?" asked Donna.

"Robert Rice," said George. Donna was shocked he could remember.

Over the next few weeks, George made great strides, saying things that gave Donna hope her husband truly was remembering and beginning to actually process his thoughts. One time he was in the shop listening to music on the Sirius XM radio 50s station and blurted out to Donna, "Imagine if there was a song with the ability to heal a broken head."

*****

One song that always inspired George was *Hot Rod Lincoln—"Have you heard this story of the Hot Rod Race, when Fords and Lincolns was settin' the pace? That story is true, I'm here to say; I was drivin' that Model A."* The song was originally written by Charlie Ryan and recorded and released in 1955. When George heard that song again, after his brain lesions, he listened to all the words, and when it came to the most iconic line—*Son, you're gonna drive me to drinkin' if you don't stop drivin' that Hot Rod Lincoln!*—the words came back to him and he sang along, remembering to pause for a beat or two between Hot-Rod-Lincoln. His memory was indeed coming back; slowly it was starting to come back.

*****

There really was a "Hot Rod Lincoln." Charlie Ryan rebuilt a car with the body of a Model A coupe set into the frame of a 1941 Lincoln. The frosting on the cake was a hopped-up Lincoln engine block. However, the song George was familiar with—had heard thousands of times, maybe more—was the cover version by Commander Cody and His Lost Planet Airmen. It would be the band's only big hit, becoming a national anthem of choice for hot rod enthusiasts around the country.

*****

George and Tootie were in the shop and Jerry Lee Lewis was performing on Sirius XM radio, banging on the piano and wailing hot licks from *Great Balls of Fire*. Donna walked in to find George standing in front of his tool box with the drawers open wide. He was digging through the tools. Donna asked, "What are you doing?"

George turned toward her and rested a hand on the valve cover of the big block. "I can't figure out how things are supposed to go together because I don't know how they came apart. I figure if I take everything apart, and put it back together, then I'll know. I'm going to tear this engine down and rebuild it."

Another song came on—Elvis Presley singing *Are You Lonesome Tonight?*—and George grinned and asked Donna, "Wanna dance?" They danced.

*****

Donna handed wrenches and drivers and sockets to George. He worked on the engine, and when he became confused, or was not sure of how things fit, he stared at the part. Tootie might come near and stand beside George, sometimes she even leaned against him. It just took time for George to sort through things in his mind. His thought process was not linear, did not follow a prescribed pattern, and sometimes jumped ahead or took a side road. Given enough time, George could eventually figure out the problem he was having.

*****

With Donna's help, George tore down and rebuilt the big block engine. Three times he tore down the engine and rebuilt it. They worked together, as a team. Then they worked to modify the frame, narrow the rear end, lengthen and widen the front end, and weld on a roll pan. They incorporated air ride and bent sheets of raw steel to manufacture custom running boards. They modified the front fenders, added several inches to the width, removed the wing windows and installed power windows all the way around. They filled, sanded and primed. They did everything to the car except for actually installing the glass and fabricating the upholstery. And while they worked, George listened to the early day rock and roll music and he got his mind right.

*****

The rock and roll that George was hearing had its roots in the rhythm and blues of the Deep South. It was said that Chuck Berry invented rock and roll. He was a black man playing black music, but times were changing and the music industry understood there was money to be made from rhythm and blues. It had nothing to do with striving to overcome social prejudice, or breaking down racial barriers, and everything to do with capitalism and profit. The music industry began promoting mainly white singers singing black music. The youth of America were in a rebellious mood, and much to their parents' chagrin, they listened to Elvis, Fats, Jerry Lee, Buddy and Little Richard. There were the Everly Brothers and the guitar licks of Duane Eddy and as the 50s melted into the 60s the folk singers drowned out rock and roll with songs about civil rights and the Vietnam War. When Bob Dylan, arguably the most influential musician of that era, led the charge against the establishment with his simple, poetic songs, George tuned out. He returned to the songs he grew up with; the rock and roll the kids had played as they cruised K Street in their souped-up hot rods. For the most part George ignored the Mersey Beat bands coming out of England—the Beatles, Rolling Stones, Yardbirds and the Animals. Psychedelic rock? Forget it. But out of the wave of changing music, George did make an exception for the Beach Boys and their free-wheeling surfer lifestyle. The music was rock and roll, but with doo-wop and sophisticated vocal harmonies. The Beach Boys song George most identified with was *Little Deuce Coupe*.

Well I'm not braggin' babe so don't put me down
But I've got the fastest set of wheels in town
When something comes up to me he don't even try
Cause if I had a set of wings man I know she could fly

She's my little deuce coupe
You don't know what I got
My little deuce coupe
You don't know what I got

Just a little deuce coupe with a flat head mill
But she'll walk a Thunderbird like it's standin' still
She's ported and relieved and she's stroked and bored
She'll do a hundred and forty with the top end floored

She's my little deuce coupe
You don't know what I got
My little deuce coupe
You don't know what I got

*****

Two of George's buddies and hot rod enthusiasts, Keith Stotts and Lee Stillwell, came from Klamath Falls to help George put the finishing touches on his car. The first time George was alone with Keith he turned to him and said, "You look really familiar. Do I know you?"

"Yeah," said Keith. "We're friends."

Working together the three men put the body together and mounted the engine. They fired it up and George drove. He circled the dry lake and when he pulled back into the shop, Donna was waiting for him. George, his eyes misty and his voice quaking, told her, "This, this is the day I've been waiting for; waiting for a long, long time."

"I know," said Donna. "I've been waiting too."

Jeanne and Jonathan

Chapter Eight

George and Donna avoided discussing the obvious fact that a person had died so that George might live. All they knew about the donor was when a doctor misguidedly made mention that George was getting the heart of a 21-year-old. George never brought up the subject because he did not know what to say; how to put his feelings of sympathy and gratitude into words. Donna never mentioned the organ donor because she still saw George as fragile. She did not wish to engage him in an emotional discussion. Then one day they received a letter from the donor's mother. At first Donna did not know what she should do. She could put the letter away and forget it, or she could meet this head on just like she had done with every other obstacle. She chose to read the letter out loud to George.

Dear Heart Recipient,

I hope this letter finds you well and happy. My name is Jeanne Hancock, and I am the mother of your heart donor. I have wanted to write to you for some time, but found it difficult.

I thought perhaps you might want to know a little bit about the person who is now a part of you. His name is Jonathan Ashley Thomas Brown. He was 21. He was in school and studying to become an electrical engineer, but his real passion was writing and fire fighting (his dad convinced him the fire fighter degree was more practical.)

Jonathan loved hiking, snowboarding, music of all kinds, laughing, writing, lively debates and hanging out with friends and family. He was caring, thoughtful, and a sweet son and a true and generous friend. Throughout school, his teachers commented that he would not tolerate injustice, and would stand up for fellow students who were being bullied. This trait is one that I am most proud of.

I have read studies, which show that some heart recipients tend to take on traits of their donor, so I was wondering if you now have a passion for large glasses of milk, and bacon cheeseburgers. Jonathan would drink almost a gallon of milk a day and polish off burgers and fries as most young adults do.

I want you to know that I am grateful that so many people and their families have benefited from Jonathan's personal choice to be an organ donor. Some family members tried to talk him out of it, but he was steadfast in his decision. It is bittersweet, but somehow gives more meaning to Jonathan's death.

I would like to correspond with you, and hope to meet you next year at the "Celebration of Life" on April 24th, 2010. If you choose not to be in contact, I completely understand. I imagine it might also be hard for you.

Know that I think of you often, and wish only the best for you, and your family.

With love and understanding,
Jeanne Hancock

*****

The social worker at OHSU who coordinates the program between organ recipients and the families of the donors was the one who forwarded the letter from Jeanne Hancock to George. After reading the letter, and looking at the photos Jeanne had enclosed showing her son, Jonathan—he was such a handsome young man and in the photographs looked so full of life—Donna asked George what he thought.

George was silent for a long moment as he fought to put his feelings into words, but the words were fleeting. He thought of *appreciative, grateful* and *thankful* but those words were so totally inadequate. George thought about the incredible pain involved in losing a child, and how difficult it must have been for Jeanne to follow Jonathan's decision to be a donor. What 21-year-old elects to become a donor? That act in itself made Jonathan a hero in George's estimation. Here was a young man who had made a conscious choice that if something terrible happened to him, others would benefit. George wished he would have had the opportunity to meet the young man. He was sure he would have liked him.

Jeanne had written that not all the family members wanted to follow through and have Jonathan's organs harvested. Jeanne must have been the one to make that final decision. How did she find the strength that such an act must have taken? George had so many questions he wanted to ask Jeanne.

Donna sat beside George on the sofa as he wrestled with his thoughts. George blurted out, "I want to call her."

Donna reached out and touched George's hand. She said, "This is an emotional time for all of us, and it must be for Jeanne too. Let's wait a few days."

*****

George thought about what he would say when he did talk to Jeanne. He would thank her for writing the letter and say how much the letter had meant to him. He would compliment her for raising such a fine son and thank her for Jonathan's heart. Of course he would thank her, and say how inadequate a thank you was; how he could never begin to express the depth of his appreciation. He searched in vain for a word more meaningful and expressive than *appreciation*. He would say how sorry he was for Jeanne's loss. No, that sounded trite. So many emotions boiled inside George: gratitude, appreciation, sadness, gratefulness, admiration and even wonderment. He wanted to say he would forever be indebted to the young man he never met. He wanted to say he felt blessed and honored to have Jonathan's heart pumping blood through his body. He wanted to say how much he admired Jonathan, a 21-year-old, for having the presence of mind—and in knowing the value to others—to become an organ donor. And he wanted to commend Jeanne for the courage it took for her to follow through with her son's wishes.

*****

George did call Jeanne. He told her his name and said he was Jonathan's heart recipient. There was a long pause and then Jeanne took a deep breath and said, "I'm glad to be able to talk to you, George."

The conversation did not go at all the way George had rehearsed it in his mind. He told Jeanne how well he was doing, said the transplant went well and that the operation took only half as long as it normally took. He said how much stronger he felt and mentioned his brain lesions, but only in passing, and then he asked, "Tell me about Jonathan."

Jeannie started slowly, saying, "He was living in Los Gatos, California with his father and stepmother when the accident happened. He was going to college." She paused and began again. "As soon as I heard about the accident—I live in Wisconsin—I caught the next flight to California. When I got there, Jonathan was still breathing on his own. That gave us hope. Then he quit breathing and the doctors put him on life support. We still had hope. We prayed and prayed. Jonathan's organs began shutting down and the doctor came to me and said if we were going to harvest the organs, now was the time to harvest them. It was the hardest decision I will ever have to make, but my son had signed the donor card—he believed in the donor program—and I felt if that was his wish, we needed to honor it."

Jeanne said other recipients were given Jonathan's organs and that she had written letters to each and every one of them, but George had been the only one who had responded. She caught George off guard when she asked, "I'm curious, since your operation, do you suddenly crave bacon cheeseburgers with the works?"

George could tell Jeannie was smiling through her tears. He knew what she wanted to hear—reports claimed some recipients took on the traits of the donor—but he had to be honest. "I love bacon cheeseburgers with the works. But then again, I always have."

*****

The following week George received a manila envelope from Jeanne. It included a letter, Jonathan's obituary, several more photographs of him, and a CD of Jonathan's favorite song, Bob Marley's *Three Little Birds*.

Dear George,

We are approaching the second anniversary of Jonathan's passing and I wanted to tell you the details of what happened. He died as the result of a car accident. The accident occurred on October 17, 2008. He was only three miles from home—the home he shared with his father, Peter, and stepmother, Lois, in Los Gatos, California. It was very late, and Jonathan's friends said he wanted to go home and sleep in his own bed. The way home is on a dark and curvy road with a number of slow corners. The police think that Jon fell asleep, and crossed over the center line, hitting another car, and then into a tree. Two boys—21 and 28, were in the other car. They had broken bones, but nothing life threatening. Jon's situation was, of course, much worse. Peter and I had given Jon the money he needed to buy a car from Peter's mom. It was a fire-engine red 1987 Mazda RX-7. To my great regret, because I did not know a car that old did not have an airbag. Jon was airlifted to the best trauma center in Northern California. Jon's ID was lost in the crash, so Peter didn't get notified until 11:30 a.m. He called me from the hospital at 3:30 p.m. Central time. I was on a plane by 7:30 p.m. that evening.

George stopped reading. Learning the details seemed almost too personal, too heartbreaking. George did not know if he felt sympathy for Jeanne, or guilt for having Jonathan's heart beating strongly in his chest. After all, Jonathan had been robbed of what every young man his age fully expected to have—the chance to go to college, meet a nice girl, date for a while, see if the two of you are compatible, fall in love, discuss the big issues like whether to have a dog or a cat, who gets to shower first in the morning while there is still plenty of hot water, and how the household chores will be divided—and if both parties are in agreement they get married, have a long career and retire. George took a breath, exhaled and kept reading.

Jon's body suffered from a massive head injury, broken ribs, arm and leg. One of his lungs was badly damaged, but the heart was in good shape. Really good shape. The doctors told us there was no hope of recovery as there was no brain activity. He was however, still breathing on his own.

It was then that we discovered that Jon was registered as an organ donor. Jon had talked with Peter about becoming a donor, and even though Peter discouraged him from doing it, Jon was very passionate and committed to the donor program. I think we all had preconceived notions about the donor process, and I must say that I was very vigilant and somewhat protective over Jon and wanted to make sure that they wouldn't just take him from us. It was such a surreal and hard time. The donor network people were good and kind people and told us the details of how it worked. If we decided that we did not want his organs removed they would leave it at that. It was Jon's choice though, so we decided to honor it. As Jon was still breathing on his own I was holding onto the possibility that he would come out of it OK. I have a network of friends who are spiritual practioners and Jon was receiving prayers from around the world. I had faith, and great hopes that he would pull through. I truly believed in the power of prayer, and still do.

Peter, Lois and I had been in the hospital for nearly two days and decided to go home for some rest. We received a call from the nurse caring for Jon on the trauma ward. She told us that we should come to the hospital right away. Jon was breathing erratically. We were with Jon when he took his last breath on his own. He was placed on a respirator and the machine did the breathing for him.

In order for his organs to be removed, Jon's vitals needed to be stabilized. It was another day of waiting. Finally everything looked good. The heart doctors—I believe there were six of them—had arrived and we were told they intended to remove the heart and immediately send it to Portland to perform the transplant surgery. Our family walked beside Jonathan as he was wheeled down the long hall, and we sang his favorite lullaby, "Three Little Birds" by Bob Marley. I kept singing as my boy was taken through the swinging doors to the surgery room. That is probably the hardest thing I have ever had to do. I wanted to keep touching him, but I knew that someone like you, George, was in desperate need and that I had to let go.

George, I do not want you to ever feel bad or sorry. It is my great privilege to have been Jonathan's mother. I am thankful that I was able to witness the man that he was becoming. I am very proud of him. I know that Jon doesn't want me to be sad, and I will never be without him. I just can't be with him physically. While writing this has been hard to do, it is also very therapeutic. I hope that this isn't too hard for you.

I have attached the obit that Peter wrote, more photos of Jon and a copy of Bob Marley singing "Three Little Birds." I hope you don't have any trouble downloading these files. The song is a bit large.

Take care and know my thoughts are with you.

Jeanne

*****

Tootie came into the room as George slipped the CD into the player. The sounds of reggae music filled the room, along with the carefree words—*this is my message to you; don't worry 'bout a thing, every little thing gonna be alright*—and the upbeat Bob Marley tune made Tootie wiggle her long neck. The image coming to George was of the family singing that song one last time as Jonathan was wheeled into the operating room so his heart could be removed and sent to Portland to be placed in George's chest. A modern miracle had completed its wide arc, and Tootie came over and laid her head on George's lap.

Don't worry about a thing
'Cause every little thing gonna be alright
Singin' don't worry about a thing
'Cause every little thing gonna be alright

Rise up this mornin'
Smiled with the risin' sun
Three little birds
Pitch by my doorstep
Singin' sweet songs
Of melodies pure and true
Sayin' this is my message to you

Singin' don't worry 'bout a thing
'Cause every little thing gonna be alright
Singin' don't worry 'bout a thing
'Cause every little thing gonna be alright

THE END

[COTY 2013]

Congratulations to George and Donna Hooker of Bonanza, Oregon. Their gorgeous 1937 Chevy Master Deluxe street rod was Hagerty's Classic of the Year for 2013, and the story of how the car came to be is amazing and inspiring. You can read it at hagerty.com/COTY13.

The Beast

The first time George fired up his '37 hot rod, heard the throaty growl of the engine and made that initial run down the highway was a very emotional day for George. That monumental event was the culmination of three decades of dedication and work. During all those years so much had happened: he had hatched a goose egg, that goose became his pet and constant companion, he had overcome debilitating health problems which included a heart transplant, and suffered with the devastating effects of brain lesions and the loss of his memory.

It was Donna, George's wife, who had been with George every step of the way; had been his strongest advocate and the one who nurtured him to regain his physical and mental health. Every day she took George to the garage, put tools in his hands, and coaxed him and challenged him to continue working on his project hot rod, the 1937 Chevy Master Deluxe Coupe. George took the big block 468 cubic inch engine completely apart and then put it back together. He did this three times and his memories, and his ability to reason and think, came back to him.

While they worked on fine-tuning the hot rod, George and Donna listened to 50s and 60s music, the rock and roll tunes from their growing-up years. Their pet goose, Tootie, supervised. The hot rod they crafted in the garage became known as *The Beast* because of the big block 468 cubic inch engine, the heartbeat of the car. They did the bulk of the work themselves, with a little help from their friends, and when they finished they entered *The Beast* in local car shows, and won every one. The crowning achievement for *The Beast* was in being named as the Hagerty's Classic Car of the Year—2013.

AWARDS FOR *THE BEAST*

Merrill Police Department Car Show
2014 Potato Festival
1st Place
1932–1940

SJS Awareness Car Show
2014
Best Car

**Kla-Mo-Ya Casino
Cruzin' Fun**
2014
1st Place

Kruise of Klamath
Modified 1935–1940
1st Place

Malin Park Car Show
Street Rod 1928 and Newer
1st Place

Hagerty's Classic Car of the Year—2013
https://www.youtube.com/watch?v=xcZstHiLdXc

DETALS – *THE BEAST*
Owners George and Donna Hooker, Bonanza, Oregon

ENGINE
468 Big Block Chevy
1965 Block and Heads
Forged Steel Crank Shaft
4-Bolt Mains
TRW Forged Pistons, 11:1 Comp. Ratio
Oil Cooler and Windage Tray

CAM
Comp Cam, Street Strip 292 H 550 Lift
Intake and Exhaust

HEADS
Oval Port, Port Matched and Blended,
Crane Roller Rockers (Lindvigs Machine)

VALVES
Stainless Steel 2.190 Intake/ 1.88 Exhaust
Comp Cams Springs

INTAKE MANIFOLD
Weiand Stealth 0-7000 Range

CARBURATOR
Holly 850 Double Pump, Cold Air Intake,
KM Filter

FUEL SYSTEM
Holly 6-Valve Marine Pump and Regulator
½ Inch Fuel Line From Fuel Cell to Carb

EXHAUST
Headman Headers, 1 7/8" Primaries
3 Inch Collectors
Collectors Extended, Equalizer Tube
2½ Inch Pipes All the Way

IGNITION
MSD 6 AL Pro-Billet Distributor
Taylor 409 Pro Race Wires

TRANS
Bud's Machine
GM Turbo 409, Swift Kit, Deep Pan, Trans Cooler
Gear Vendors Under Over Drive, Gear Splitter
Drive Shaft Loop

REAR END
Chrysler 8¾, 389 Casting, 457 Gears
Posi-Traction, 31 Spline Axles

SUSPENSION
Front: Early 70s Camaro, 2" Drop Spindle
Over-Sized Sway Bar
Rear: Alston Ladder Bar Pan Hard Bar
Front and Rear Air-Ride

WHEELS
Rear: Crager Drag Star, 15 X 15 Alum.
Front: Crager Drag Star, 4 X 15 Alum.

TIRES
Rear: 33 X 19:50 X 15
Front: 26 X 7:50 X 15
Mickey Thompson

BODY
1937 Chevy Custom Coupe Master Deluxe
All Steel

INTERIOR
Bill's Upholstery, Klamath Falls, Oregon

GLASS
Cooks Glass, Klamath Falls, Oregon

BODY MODIFICATIONS
Custom One Piece Hood With Removable Sides
V-Butt Windshield
3-Point Seatbelts
Front Fenders Widened 2 Inches, Length 3 Inches
Cutom Side Mirrors
Custom Turn Signals Front and Rear
Third Brake Light Holder Into Body
Eliminated Quarter Windows For 3 Window Coupe
Eliminate Wing Windows in Doors
Installed Power Windows
Custom Dash
Shaved Drip Rails
Custom Running Boards Widened
Rear Fenders Widened and Molded Into Body
Custom Roll Pan In Back
Deck Lid Modified For Molded In License Plate

Acknowledgements

With appreciation and special thanks to the following individuals: Mark Christensen, Terry Romero, Dianne Mathisen, Dennis Cole, Pamela Laughton Glave, Alys Means, Jaycee Fletcher-Wise, Norma McCool, Will Steber, Colleen & Dick Pedersen, Jody Conners, Kathleen Howard, Diane Tupper, Kristine Taylor, Mary Preston and Bob Cordes.

More that 3,000 people in the Northwest are currently on the donor list waiting for organ transplants that will save their lives. But a growing shortage of donors means not all those in such desperate need will receive their transplant in time.

If you chose to become a donor, you may touch over 50 lives - healing a burn victim, saving the life of a newborn with congenital heart defects, and much more. And donation isn't just about organs! Cornea donation restores sight to thousands each year.

By educating and registering people in the Pacific Northwest, Donate Life Northwest gives HOPE to all those waiting for a transplant. Please help us save lives: register as a donor, and learn more by exploring our educational resources, FAQs, and joining us through activities and events. To register, or to make a financial contribution, please call 800-452-1369, or visit www.donatelifenw.org

Leslie Brock
Executive Director
Donate Life Northwest